Butler Royal

BUTLER ROYAL

Peter Russell

HUTCHINSON
London Melbourne Sydney Auckland Johannesburg

To Leigh (Reggie) Crutchley

Hutchinson & Co. (Publishers) Ltd
An imprint of the Hutchinson Publishing Group
17–21 Conway Street, London W1P 6JD
Hutchinson Group (Australia) Pty Ltd
30–32 Cremorne Street, Richmond South, Victoria 3121
PO Box 151, Broadway, New South Wales 2007
Hutchinson Group (NZ) Ltd
32–34 View Road, PO Box 40–086, Glenfield, Auckland 10
Hutchinson Group (SA) Pty Ltd
PO Box 337, Bergvlei 2012, South Africa
First published 1982
© Peter Russell 1982
Set in VIP Sabon by
D. P. Media Limited, Hitchin, Hertfordshire
Printed in Great Britain by The Anchor Press Ltd
and bound by Wm Brendon & Son Ltd,
both of Tiptree, Essex

British Library Cataloguing in Publication Data
Russell, Peter
  Butler Royal.
  1. Russell, Peter   2. Servants – England –
  Biography
  640'.46'0924   TX331

ISBN 0 09 147850 2

ILLUSTRATIONS

My mother and I, aged three months
RAF Hednesford, nr Cannock, 1952
Aged eighteen, outside my home in Alperton, Wembley
Playing the part of the butler in Terence Rattigan's play,
  While the Sun Shines
Shirley and I on our wedding day, September 1958
The Christmas card sent to me by Princesses Marina and
  Alexandra in 1956
The Duke of Kent as a teenager
Princess Alexandra at her piano, watched by her mother
Princess Alexandra and Madame Poplewska-Koziell taking
  tea in the garden at Coppins
Arriving at Liverpool Street Station from Sandringham
The Baroness de Stoekl
The Christmas card sent by the Queen and Prince Philip to
  Princess Marina in 1957
Bear Place, Twyford, Berkshire, the home of Lord and Lady
  Remnant
Coppins
Washing-up after the Queen Mother called for tea in 1962
Signed photograph of Alice and Henry, Duke and Duchess of
  Gloucester
Signed wedding photograph of the Duke and Duchess of
  Kent, 1961

At the front door of Bear Place in 1966
The Duke and Duchess of Kent and the Earl of St Andrews
Shirley and I leaving home for Princess Alexandra's wedding
   in 1963
The drawing room at Coppins in the fifties

ONE

DUKE: Good morning, Horton.

HORTON: Good morning, your Grace.

DUKE: Pay this taxi fellow, will you? I've got no change.

HORTON: Very good, your Grace.

DUKE: Is nobody awake?

HORTON: All three young gentlemen were asleep when I went in a little while ago. I shook the shoulder nearest the wall, which I took to be his Lordship's but which proved to belong to the American gentleman. He told me to scram, which I understood to mean that they had all passed a restless night, did not wish to be disturbed and required no breakfast.

DUKE: You've heard the news, I suppose, Horton?

HORTON: About his Lordship's engagement to Miss Crum? Yes, your Grace, he told me last night.

DUKE: It's a shocking business. He seems absolutely set on it, I gather.

HORTON: I'm afraid so, your Grace. I did attempt to indicate my disapproval with one of my looks. He said it was the only way he could save himself from extinction in the postwar world.

As I spoke Horton's words from Terence Rattigan's play *While the Sun Shines* on the stage of the RAF camp cinema at Oakington, near Cambridge, I had no idea that in the near future they were to become part of my daily vocabulary, nor that they were in their way prophetic,

for, although most of my time I served in the loftiest households, I had the occasional experience of more humble homes
and so helped to 'save the upper classes from extinction'.

From the beginning I must state that the class distinction
which was then, and indeed is now, very much a part of the
social structure of this country is one that basically I accept;
but although this acceptance enabled me to work in service,
ironically it was ultimately one of my reasons for leaving. I
don't say this in criticism or out of bitterness or envy. I
accepted it easily from childhood and I have had little cause
to change either my mind or my attitude over the years.
Nowhere is this distinction more apparent than in domestic
service where it is visited not just on the servants by their
masters, but on the lesser servants by their superiors.

But back to the play. Even if I hadn't been fond of acting
for as long as I can remember, and an extrovert by nature, I
should still have volunteered to take part in it. I had begun
my National Service in 1952, doing the regulation eight
weeks' square-bashing, which shattered all my Biggles illusions of 'scrambling formation flying and air combat with the
chatter of machine-gun bullets and the reek of carbon'. Nor
indeed did my posting to the 206 Advanced Flying School at
Oakington permit any continuation of these Biggles fan-
tasies. I was given the only job that was considered open to
me, that of admin orderly. This was the lowest of the low,
and although by dint of keeping my eyes and ears open, I
eventually managed to get myself a more cushy and interesting billet, service life didn't have a lot to offer, and socially it
was a write-off.

Performing in a play seemed a cheerful distraction. The
producer, Leslie Eccles, was a flight sergeant. It took me a day
or two to find him.

'You're a bit late,' he said. 'I've cast all the parts except
one.' I must have looked a bit crestfallen. It must surely be
only a walk-on.

'It's a very good part and I've had some difficulty finding

the right person to play it. It's a chap called Horton, he's the butler. I'm sure you're just the bloke for it.'

I wasn't sure whether this was a compliment.

'Anyway, come along to rehearsals tonight and we'll see how it goes.'

I had one or two questions to ask first. 'Any officers taking part?'

'No, it's all other ranks.'

'What about girls?' We hadn't any WAAF or other women on the staff, and plays, as I had found in the past, were a fair hunting ground.

'We've got a couple from the village. There may be more working behind the scenes,' he added when he saw that I didn't feel that two would be enough to go round.

'Rehearsals?'

'In the Naafi. Seven o'clock. Don't be late.' With that he made off.

I couldn't see that any harm was likely to be done, so I presented myself as he requested. I was early, so I made myself known to those who had already arrived.

'Well, Leslie's cast the part at last,' someone said. 'We thought no one would take it.'

That wasn't exactly music to my ears. 'Why, what's wrong with it?'

'Nothing wrong with it exactly, but everyone else thought it a bit degrading to play the part of a butler, looked on it as a sort of male skivvy.'

I must have coloured up. 'I haven't decided yet whether to take the part.' This seemed to cause some rustling in the dove cotes.

'Don't take any notice of Corporal King. He's all piss and wind,' said a bloke whom I later knew as Bob Garwood and who was stage managing as well as acting. Just then Leslie Eccles arrived and we got under way. Everyone seemed quite impressed by my reading; even the two girls from the village had words of praise, but I noticed that they had already formed some sort of relationship, one with the Earl of Harpenden and the other with the Duke of Eyr and Stirling. Bloody snobs, women, I thought as I made my way back to my billet.

It was one of those shows where everything seemed to go right, even the dress rehearsal. We gave three performances, and the final night was a sort of gala occasion, with the station commander, Group Captain Ramsey Rae, in the front row with his wife, and the majority of the other officers taking up the 'orchestra stalls'. It soon became obvious that they had packed a fair amount of alcohol away beforehand for they laughed and applauded like kids at a Punch and Judy show. They came on stage afterwards, distributing beer and the like as if it were going out of fashion.

During these celebrations, Ramsey Rae approached me and drew me to one side.

'Jolly good show, Russell. You were the butler to the last. First class. Excellent.'

I wondered what was coming next. I had no illusions. All right, I was good in the part, at home in it, you might say, but so were most of the others. I could sense that something more was in the wind and I was right.

'Ahem, I'd like you to come to see me at my office at nine tomorrow morning, Russell. That OK?'

Although it didn't sound like an order, it was, and so it had to be OK.

He moved away murmuring, 'Jolly good show. Look forward to seeing you.'

I've always found it hard getting to sleep after a show and this night it was even harder, for apart from the excitement, there was the visit to the CO to contend with. I rose early, did my normal duties and got myself smartened up for the station office. I seemed to be expected. The adjutant quickly appeared, greeted me and announced me to the group captain. He was as affable as he had been the night before.

'Come on in, Russell. Shan't keep you long. Just an informal chat.'

That's what he may have thought it was, but I wasn't so sure.

'It was a bit of a coincidence seeing you on the stage last night. You won't have heard, but my batman is leaving me shortly. Been a very good fella. No complaints in that direction, but my wife and I both thought it would be a good idea if we had someone with a difference next time.'

I must have looked puzzled.

'I'll explain. We have to do a deal of entertaining at home, tea parties, dinner parties, that sort of thing. Part of the job, keeping in with the locals. So we thought it would cut a bit of a dash if we had a kind of butler to wait at the table, pour the wines, announce the guests, that sort of thing, very much like you did last night. You'd be well looked after, plenty of time off, and you'll eat the same food as we do. Matter of fact, I wouldn't mind doing the job myself.'

For the first time I experienced a feeling of disbelief. He was gilding the lily in his enthusiasm. Still, that enthusiasm was catching: butler/batman might have its advantages. I would be at the centre of things, and I could already imagine senior NCOs hanging on my words and treating me with the respect I'd never previously known or earned.

'Well, what do you say, Russell?' The group captain brought me back to earth.

'I'll give it a bash, sir, or rather I'll endeavour to give of my best, sir.'

This play on words was not lost on him, and he burst out laughing. 'I like a chap with a sense of humour. Well, that's settled then. Capital. I'm certain you won't regret it.'

'When would you like me to start, sir?'

'Let's say a week from today, but I'd like you to call on Mrs Ramsey Rae as soon as you can. She can tell you more about it than I can. You and I will be sure to see each other before you begin your duties. Well, thank you, Russell, that will be all.'

So it was that during my last year of National Service I

learned something of the rudiments of being a butler, rudiments that were shortly to stand me in good stead, and all because of a play called *While the Sun Shines*. At the risk of sounding corny, it certainly shone on me during most of my life in domestic service.

Although the play may have sparked things off, I later tried to analyse what it was that directed me into service. This meant going back over my past life. It was worthwhile, for I found a recurring theme which I think gave me the answer I was looking for.

I was born in Willesden, a rather ordinary part of north-west London, on 20 September 1933. I've never known exactly where for, when I was two years old, we moved to Alperton in Wembley, to Tiverton Road, a cul-de-sac of terraced houses. We were comfortably off by working-class standards. I had an elder brother, Edward, who was thought to be the brains of the family. Dad drove a trolley bus, while Mum looked after the home and the children. She had never been out to work since she was married. A woman didn't work in those days unless she was a spinster – a dreaded word. It was a sort of inverted snobbery. There was a snobbery amongst the working class, the same spirit of one-upmanship that there is today, but instead of fitted carpets, tumble dryers, colour television and central heating, it was new lino, net curtains and radiograms. We had our own kind of central heating. When it was freezing cold, Mum would light the oven of the gas stove and leave the door open. Then each member of the family in turn would grab his clothes and dress in the kitchen.

Dad had been brought up by Grandpa Russell, as we called him. His brother had been a kind of exalted bargee. At one time he had owned seven boats and named them after his sons. He was put out of business by road transport, but went on living in a house by the Grand Union Canal. He was a gruff old buffer, one of the old school – 'children may be seen but not heard' – and my father took after him. Mum's dad ran a laundry and washed the shirts, linen and such like for those whom we thought of as the upper class in Willesden and Cricklewood. Just as Grandpa Russell was lucky in having several sons who could help him with his boats, so Mum's dad was similarly blessed as he had four daughters. He was unfortunate with his wives though. Mum's mum died of cancer when she was very young. He tried again but his second wife died too. He'd have nothing more to do with marriage after that, but took up with a third lady much younger than himself, which was just as well as he lived to see ninety-two and she was able to nurse him to the end. His business did well and when he died, Mum and the others thought they had some expectations, but it was all left to the lady friend. Rightly, I thought, and said so.

'That's all very well,' said Mum, 'but when you went to bed as a lad, you didn't have to tie a bit of string round your big toe and have it tugged at five in the morning when your father woke, and you didn't have to be up and working over a tub half an hour later. I reckon we all deserved something for having to suffer that. Then at nights we'd be driving the horse and cart at all times and in all weathers, delivering the baskets, while he was wining and dining at some local hostelry.' I began to see her point.

Until I was seven, our family prospered within our social terms. We entertained a good deal, relations and neighbours. We owned a piano (another social distinction), and there was always someone who could pummel out a tune, so we had sing-songs and the sort of games that would be considered really boring today, but from which we derived a lot of fun. Fortune-telling was a great favourite among the women, and was taken quite seriously. I remember one great aunt who wouldn't have anyone else in the room while her fortune was being told. Nor would she speak about it afterwards. I thought that she must have some guilty secrets that she didn't want revealed, but then I remembered her face and figure; though I'd been told there was many a good tune played on an old fiddle, I doubted if such melodies were played on one with the looks of a tuba, the body of a cello and a voice like the bagpipes. Everyone was called on to make some contribution to the gaiety and I was one of the first on my feet. My forte was imitations, and judging by the cries of 'Well done, Pete,' and 'Isn't he a caution?' they seemed to be appreciated.

At school it was the same; if we were asked to recite or appear in a concert, I was always there at the top of the queue. The appreciation of the staff wasn't quite the same as I got at home. 'Just as well you're good at something, Russell, eh, my boy?' was generally the comment. I was neither bright nor hard-working.

Then came the war. Like most other London children, I was evacuated. I went to Chesham in Buckinghamshire, not very far, but it seemed like going to Australia. I wasn't happy there and after three months of the phoney war I went back home.

It was as well that I did, for Dad was taken ill and as Mum had to nurse him, she was glad of the extra pair of hands around the place. Eventually he was taken to hospital, where he died. He didn't leave any money, so plans had to be made. We let half the house, and my brother, who was now in the RAF, was able to help out, but there still wasn't enough, so Mum had to go out to work. She got a job doing something she knew about and enjoyed, cooking in a works canteen. She started early in the mornings, so I had to look after myself, make my bed, prepare breakfast and, giving the place a lick and a polish, get myself to school. I was home before Mum, so I was able to do a variety of household jobs to make life easier for her. I wasn't an exception: a lot of kids whose fathers were in the forces were having to do the same thing.

When the daylight raids started we had our lessons in an air-raid shelter and we spent many nights in one until we got our own Morrison shelter. If it got really noisy in the night,

we would start a sing-song to take our minds off things, and I
would be called upon to do a turn when I was hardly able to
keep my eyes open.

My worst bomb experience happened one day when I was
coming back from school. The alert had scarcely sounded
when the bombs started to fall. Suddenly I was grabbed from
behind. I turned to see a little old woman. 'Come on in, son.
It's too dangerous for you to be out on the streets.' I did as I
was told and was bundled into a gap under the stairs. She sat
at my side, with a Persian cat on her lap and holding a cage
containing four budgerigars. I forgot all about the raid as I
watched the cat's green eyes: he was mentally devouring
those poor birds. From the way they fluttered around, I could
tell they weren't keen on the situation either. I still have
nightmares about it.

I wasn't afraid during the air raids as long as Mum was by
my side. The noise took a bit of getting used to at first; indeed,
it increased as more and more anti-aircraft guns went into
action. We were comparatively lucky, at any rate during the
early years of the war, with only the occasional stick of
bombs dropping near us; our windows remained intact until
1943.

It was about then that I fell in love for the first time. Violet
was in the same class as me at school, and although we
exchanged the odd glance or note, we had to be careful, for if
any of my pals found out, I'd have been ragged unmercifully,
and life wouldn't have been worth living. When the alert
sounded, things were different: as the noise drew nearer,
Violet's hand would find mine. I think she was genuinely
afraid, but I almost hoped Jerry would fly overhead and she
would fling her arms around me. I could imagine myself
rescuing her from a heap of rubble and thus winning her
undying love. I never knew what her real feelings about me
were. We used to walk home from school together with our
fingers occasionally touching and she told me how much she
enjoyed my performances. Then we would go to the pictures

together. We couldn't afford to pay, so we would wait by the exit doors and walk in when someone came out. I would tell her how I was going to be an actor when I grew up, embellishing my future life with bits I had read in movie magazines. The awful day came when she broke the news that her family was moving, not very far, Brentford I think it was, but it sounded like the end of the world. We looked at maps and worked out where we could meet halfway, but it never came to anything, and I was left with a broken heart and a medallion of St Christopher which I have kept to this day. I didn't give her anything except a kiss on the lips, which was the first and last we were to exchange.

The worst of the Blitz came towards the end of 1943 when Goering stepped up his bombing of British towns and cities. Our street escaped but those surrounding us were hit and an oil bomb flattened a large area. It did us a power of no good at all. All the windows were blasted and the front and back doors hung drunkenly on their hinges. The place was in chaos. When Mum saw what had happened she flopped into a chair with her head in her hands and cried her eyes out. She didn't know how or where to begin.

It was our next-door neighbour – 'Ma Hawkings' we called her – who came to the rescue. She had only moved in a couple of years earlier when she lost her home and her left arm in a raid in the Old Kent Road. Despite the fact that her place must have been as bad as the neighbours', she went around cheering everyone up. When she saw how badly Mum was taken, she got her onto her feet. 'Come on, ducks, let's get started. You'll be surprised how little damage has been done once you start sweeping up and dusting around.' She thrust a broom into Mum's hands and, taking one herself, began on what looked like all the labours of Hercules put together.

She was a wonderful woman, Ma Hawkings; she could do more with one arm than a gang of navvies. I felt I was in the way and, wanting to see where the bombs had dropped, I cut away. First I visited the houses where my friends lived. The first couple were no worse off than we were. Then I saw Derek Merrifield's place. It had had a direct hit. I think it was at that moment that I realized the full force of the war. I began sobbing. I was certain no one could have lived under the rubble.

'You a relation or something?' I heard a voice ask.

'Just a friend.'

'Well, you'll be glad to know the family went to stay with relations a couple of nights ago. There was no one in the house when the bomb dropped.'

I didn't continue on my travels; the shock and the relief were too much for me. I made my way back home, which, as Ma Hawkings had predicted, was beginning to look like something again, and I set to and gave a helping hand.

The doodle-bugs came and went, adding new perils and new experiences. Many people found them more frightening than the bombs. I did when they first started, then one night Mum and I went to the theatre to see Ivor Novello's *The Dancing Years*. During one of the scenes we heard a doodle-bug approaching; it drew nearer and for a few seconds it seemed as though it was heading directly for us. I could almost hear the audience breathe a sigh of relief as it passed over. That was one of the things about doodle-bugs – we always selfishly wished them on someone else. On stage the cast carried on as if nothing was happening, so from then on I determined to do the same. 'If you want to be an actor, you've got to behave like one' became part of my creed.

The end of the war in Europe was a red-letter day in everyone's calendar, but the one that shines out most at that time was the day the street held its VE party. Except in posh areas every street had them, fortunately on different days, otherwise heaven knows where we would have got the bunting from that was festooned across from house to house. There was, of course, a committee, to which I was coopted. I was given the job of organizing the entertainment for the fourteen-year-olds and under. I have been on committees since but never on one where any idea had such universal support. In fact, there was only one near disagreement. Two next-door neighbours both offered their radiograms to provide the music and each declared that theirs was the louder and of better quality. Things looked like turning nasty, until the chairman suggested using both, one at one end of the street and one at the other.

I was kept busy arranging dances for the little ones, writing scripts, recruiting and training what talent we had for the rest. The mums of course made the costumes and the fancy dresses. Where the money came from heaven alone knows, but it was a real slap-up do that went on all day. Where the food came from was easier to understand. Some households had been conserving stuff for just such a day. There were others whose members worked in shops and either bartered the goods they sold for food or, if they happened to be working in food shops, dropped boxes of biscuits or dented tins of meat or fish so they were unsalable. Others, generally the most fruitful, picked up stuff that had fallen off the back of a lorry.

Everything went with a swing, including the entertainments I had organized. The mayor and mayoress of Wembley, wearing their chains of office, arrived in a large Daimler. I was astonished that there was no drunkenness, particularly as the beer was on the house, as it were. Blokes that I had seen reeling home on a Saturday night were as good as gold, maybe because their wives were keeping an eye on them. Everyone voted it the best party ever, and some suggested that it should be made a regular event, but within only a few weeks the peeping through curtains and back-biting started again.

Another event at this time that I shall always remember was the Saturday afternoon of the Cup Final. Instead of going out with my pals, I decided to watch the King and Queen as they drove past the end of the street. Although Mum, and in his day, Dad, were rank Labour, they were royalists, and this had brushed off onto me, particularly because of the way the royal family had behaved during the war. I even kept a scrapbook of their travels, both in London and around the country.

A big crowd gathered at the end of the street and I noticed that many of those who had said they wouldn't cross the road to see them were down there in front. I stood waiting with my flag at the ready and a feeling of excitement rising in my belly. First the traffic stopped. Two motorcycle outriders appeared, then the royal Rolls with the King and Queen. The Queen sat well forward, waving at the crowd. I felt as if she were waving to me personally and flailed my flag backwards and forwards as if my life depended on it. It was all over in a matter of seconds, yet then, and as I write about it now, it seemed so much longer. After their disappearance, all was anticlimax. The Duke of Gloucester followed in another Rolls, but he didn't seem to notice that we were there. 'Looks like a grumpy old sod,' I murmured to whoever was standing next to me. How strange to think that in a few years' time I would be a senior member of his domestic staff, his butler.

When I was fifteen, I left school with little optimism about the future, either from the masters, my mother or myself. There was only one thing I wanted to do, but I knew there was little chance I would get the opportunity. Mum had never encouraged my love of theatre. To her it was just so much pie in the sky. It was with some surprise and not much enthusiasm, therefore, that I received a letter from our school's careers master, telling me that if I felt so inclined, I could go and see the appointments officer at Simpson's, Piccadilly, and that he might have something for me. I thought I had better go along and case the joint before coming to any decision. I was delighted with what I saw. It was a sort of miniature Harrods, specializing in clothes for the upper-middle classes. It wasn't your Savile Row tailor, your Lobs or your Hawes and Curtis. A lot of what they sold was off the peg, but to me it was, and indeed still is, a classy establishment. I went inside. I was able to wander about at will: no one accosted me. A quick glance must have convinced them that there was no money coming from my direction. I was amazed at the smartness and efficiency of the staff and I kept looking at the customers, thinking I might see some film personality. It was just the sort of place I could imagine them using.

I duly wrote a letter of application, dressed myself up and went along for inspection and interrogation by the appointments officer. All must have gone well for I received a letter a few days later telling me to report for duty the following Monday, that I would be classed as a trainee salesman and would receive 35s. a week and a free lunch. I gave Mum £1 out of this, my fares were 5s. and the rest was my own. It was certainly a far cry from an actor's life, but for a lad like me it had a certain glamour, and learning about good clothes was later to prove of great value.

For the first six months I spent one day a week with the training officer and during that time was given the basis of tailoring and the care of clothes. I learned how to brush them, how to fold them and particularly how to pack them, because whenever one of the assistants made a sale, the clothes were handed to me to box and to do up in a parcel worthy of the name of the house of Simpson. After my training I had hopes of making a sale, and so proving myself worthy of my title, but I rarely got the opportunity. There were three salesmen senior to me who stepped forward and took over even if I had started chatting up a customer. The only fun I seemed to get was on a quiet day when the other salesmen went for their tea and I was left in charge. Then I would grab some jackets and overcoats, make for a cubicle and doll myself up. 'This is how I'll look one of these days,' I promised myself.

One of the first things I discovered, to my surprise, was the number of dramatic societies there were in central London, all of which seemed to be short of young men. I was really a bit too young, but with the male scarcity I got by. This, as I had hoped, brought me and girls together, but not with the results I was looking for: I might satisfy as a juvenile, but off stage I wasn't thought of as a Romeo.

I'd been at Simpson's some nine months when I ran into trouble. It happened during one of our quiet periods and I was on my own. A proper toff came over. He was wearing what I now recognize as a Savile Row suit and the rest of his outfit went along with it.

'I'm looking for a camel-hair coat. My tailor, it seems, will take too long to make one. Do you think that one over there will fit?'

I tried it on him and it suited a treat.

'I'll take it. You needn't bother to wrap it up, I'll wear it now. Have it put down to my account, will you?'

'What name shall I say?'

He raised an eyebrow as if he was surprised I didn't know. 'Rutland, Lord Rutland.'

Well, I fawned. He was the first titled gent I had met. 'Yes, m'Lord. Thank you, m'Lord. Sign here, m'Lord.'

He did, and was out of the shop in a trice, leaving me ten bob for my trouble. After I'd recovered from the shock, I rang through to accounts. The moment I mentioned his name, a voice at the other end said, 'Oh, Christ, not again. Is he still there?'

I stammered out what had happened.

'Why didn't you check with us before parting with the coat. It's routine. You've been conned, you bloody little fool. Well, get back to work. You'll be for the high jump tomorrow.'

At home that night I worked out how long it would take to earn enough money to pay for the coat. I think I went to sleep counting pound notes. But, although I was rocketed by one of the store's directors, there was no mention of payment or dismissal. I wasn't the only one to have been trapped and, with a final warning of 'Never judge a sausage by its skin', he dismissed me. I wasn't so well treated when I got back to the department. My leg was pulled by some of the juniors, and the senior salesman's eyes never seemed to leave me. In a way I was lucky. I still had the 10s. 'his Lordship' had given me. I hadn't thought it necessary to mention that little matter. Well, when I first joined Simpson's I had hoped to meet some members of the acting profession. 'Lord Rutland' was the only one I did and, by God, he turned in a good performance.

Now rising seventeen, I had just over twelve months before I would be called up to do my two-year period of National Service. I couldn't see myself getting anywhere at Simpson's after my fall from grace, so I decided to look around for another job. It had to be in central London because of my theatrical commitments. I was lucky. I applied for a job as a junior office clerk to a razor-blade company called Pal. I got £1 a week more than I got at Simpson's for being no more than a glorified office boy. I made the tea, packed parcels and often delivered them. Filing, sorting out invoices – you name it, I did it. The thing that astonished me about this job was that whatever I was called upon to do, someone always said thank you. And the girls began to notice me. I got romantic notions about one in particular, but another bloke with prospects came along and I was quietly discarded.

As office boy, I was in the position of learning more about the various facts of life than most boys of my age. I moved around so much, I could see everything that was going on and, probably because I was young, the staff would confide in me. In fact it got so that I was treated as a sort of social and sexual encyclopedia. 'If you want to know anything about that, you'd best ask Peter.'

It was while I was with Pal that I met a few theatricals. Our offices were in Mount Street where there were a number of flats and it also led into a fashionable area. I got autographs from Trevor Howard, Kathleen Harrison, Robert Morley and the like. One day, bursting out of the office (I always moved fast going in or out, it gave a good impression), I bumped straight into Valerie Hobson, nearly knocking her over. I apologized profusely, and then, recognizing her, congratulated her on her performance in the film *Great Expectations*. She was a real lady and asked me what I did for a living. I told her and added that I would really like to be an actor. This made her laugh. Then, with the cheek of the working class, I said how much I would like to visit a film studio. She gave me her card with an address on it in Mount Street, told me to phone her in a few days, and she would see what could be arranged. She was as good as her word and a fortnight later I had a 'grandmother's funeral' and visited Pinewood Studios. I was taken round the various stages, given lunch in the canteen, and by the end of the day was a deal wiser about what went on in the film world. It decided me to enlist at a crowd agency.

I knew you had to take photos with you, so I went along with everything I could lay my hands on. I got a big laugh for this from the girl who was registering my name. 'You're the first person to come here with a photo in a frame.' I think it was that bit of stupidity that got my first job in a Robert Donat film, *The Magic Box*. This meant two days' sick leave and I came out of it eight quid the richer.

It was my first and last appearance, for a fortnight later I received my call-up papers for National Service with the RAF.

I continued my office-boy duties in the orderly room, though now I was the lowest of the low, and no one ever said thank you for anything; but I was at the centre of things, so when there was a job going in the officers' mess, I was able to get my name in first. As I hadn't made any recognizable contributions to the running of the office, no difficulties were put in my way. I was accused of skiving by Warrant Officer Kettle, but I'd been on the receiving end of gratuitous insults from him since I joined. I reckoned I could take that, and anything else he was likely to throw at me. He was a bugger about hair, always accusing me of wearing mine too long. I got so fed up I thought I'd give him more than he bargained

for and had what they called then a 'brush cut' with my hair
sticking up a quarter of an inch all over.

When Kettle saw it, he said, 'What's the matter with you,
Russell? Got alopecia or something?'

I didn't know what the hell he was talking about, so I said
'No, Warrant Officer. I had that when I was a kid.' It was the
first and last time I saw him laugh.

The job in the officers' mess was as batman/waiter. I had six
officers to look after, take their morning tea, make their beds,
clean and brush their uniforms. Six was a lot to take care of,
and they didn't always get the full treatment. Still, nobody
grumbled. It was more than most of them were used to in
civvy street. A number of them were on short-service com-
missions, training to fly Meteor 7 jets. I must have put a jinx
on them for during the nine months I was in the mess I lost
four officers, all killed in crashes. News of this got round, so
that when a new officer joined and was asked who was
looking after him, he was brought an extra drink for luck. It
wasn't a pleasant reputation to have.

By the time I had seen to the officers and their quarters, it
was about eleven o'clock. I would snatch a cup of tea and
then make myself useful in the kitchen or pantry, wherever I
was directed. At midday we sat down to our lunch, then
quickly cleared that, and were standing by at 12.45 when
some of the sixty officers began trickling in for theirs. Then
came the rush as the drinkers swallowed up and descended
on us before we put the shutters up. From then on it was all
bustle and go. Corporals and leading aircraftmen served the
main dish, while I and the other AC1s followed with the
vegetables and sauces, clearing the first course plates as we
went. The food was straightforward; the officers didn't like it
'nanced around', as they were quick to tell the mess secretary.

Lunch over and cleared, we had a couple of hours to
ourselves, followed by the same routine for dinner, though
we didn't have to cater for so many as a lot of officers took
themselves off to Cambridge. There was, though, one mess

night a week when attendance was compulsory and ladies'
and guest nights at least once a month, when some visiting
senior officer or local dignitary would be guest of honour
(ladies were often allowed at these dos as well). Such occasions were welcome since they could provide a source of
income. If any officer kept his lady friend with him for the
night, there was the accepted rate of £1 as 'silence money'.
Some officers managed to smuggle their totties in on ordinary
nights, so it paid well to have a randy officer or two. It was
very different for the NCOs and airmen. We had our own
regular dances, but partners were brought in from surrounding towns and villages by coach and were accounted for by
some sort of matron when they filed out for the journey back.
Relationships had to be established quickly and any heavy
snogging could only take place on the lawns outside the
Naafi.

I enjoyed the officers' dining-in nights for we were dolled
up in white jackets with gold buttons, stiff collars, starched
shirts and bow ties; drink flowed freely and everyone let their
hair down. As often as not I would be on the door to
announce the guests; to me it was all play-acting.

Although for disciplinary matters we came under a flight
sergeant, I was lucky that the civilian steward, Tom Betts,
took an interest in me. He saw that I was keen on the job and
went out of his way to encourage me. He varied my duties so
that I got to know a little about most things. When he felt I
was ready, he recommended me for bar work, which meant
promotion and more money. I learned to chat with the
officers and, although the drinks available were those found
in any ordinary pub, I learned how to tap and keep a barrel
of beer and became proficient with a few mixed drinks. So
when it came to Group Captain Rae asking me to join him as
his butler, it wasn't just the play that prompted him. He
already knew my background; I have always suspected that
Tom Betts had something to do with my promotion,
although he would never admit it.

Strangely I didn't learn much about being a butler while I was with the CO, but I did learn how a middle-class family lived and behaved, and a great deal more about food, its selection, preparation and cooking, for their Irish chef, O'Grady, inevitably called Paddy, and I struck up an easy relationship. His jollity and easy-going manner was infectious, though I'm glad to say I never caught his unending capacity for the drink. There was also a cleaning woman who came up each day from the village and kept us up to date with local gossip.

Apart from the CO we only had his wife and mother-in-law to look after, so my duties were light, though Paddy would complain that it was just as easy to cook for half a dozen, and sometimes a damn sight easier as it allowed him greater scope. The house was run by the CO's mother-in-law, Mrs Howell. It proved a happy arrangement, leaving Mrs Rae free to think about her looks and her clothes. She played the part expected of a commanding officer's wife, entertaining the wives of other officers. She was spoken of as a 'tower of strength' so she must have done her job well. She always seemed to know when other ranks' wives or children were visiting and would run into them by design and make them feel welcome.

My day now began early: up at 6.30 and over to the house by seven for shoe-cleaning and button-polishing. Then I would prepare the tea trays, which Paddy took up. Breakfast was at eight, and I would be waiting in the hall at 8.25 to give the group captain his hat and cane and hand him over to his driver. He was always on parade, as it were, by 8.30.

After breakfast, mother-in-law came into the kitchen to give the orders of the day. She was a largish lady with a precise voice, enunciating every word, which was something I had learned from my acting. After provisioning had been attended to, I cleaned the silver, pressed the CO's uniform for the following day and his evening wear if he was either entertaining officially or being entertained that night. I then laid up lunch, served it, and Paddy and I shared the washing-up. We were both free in the afternoon until 5.30 when we began preparing for dinner. This was the same routine unless we had guests, when I had to work at double speed. After we had finished clearing up, Paddy, who had a home and a wife in the village, would ride his bike at break-neck speed to the pub. The effects of the time he spent there were usually apparent the following day.

One task I have never forgotten was feeding the chickens, of which the Ramsey Raes kept a quantity. I also collected the eggs, which wasn't as easy as it sounds, since the birds were free range and laid in the most unlikely places. If we were having chicken for supper, mother-in-law would come with me, pick out a likely 'lamb for the slaughter' and together we would try to catch it. If it had a particularly sad look, I wouldn't cooperate, and another would have to be chosen. Mrs Howell tried to teach me how to wring a chicken's neck. I couldn't do that and after several fruitless attempts, she kept the role of executioner. It is all right for someone brought up in the country, but for a townie like me it seemed murder.

Being the CO's batman/butler meant I had gone up in the social scale. On guest nights I now served at the top table and was treated with some respect by my colleagues, no matter their rank. This applied in particular to Warrant Officer Kettle. Apparently it meant a great deal for him to know precisely what the station commander's movements were going to be. Kettle would seek me out, knowing that I knew. At first I was free with my information, but eventually began to tease him by being uncertain. I think he knew what I was at, but he couldn't do anything about it, lest the source dry up completely. I got him fawning, and if ever I wanted anything which needed his help, it was forthcoming. It was playing this cat-and-mouse game which gave me the greatest pleasure during my time with the Ramsey Raes.

Eventually the day for my demob drew near. Frankly, I

was happy that my National Service was coming to an end though, like anyone who has had a spell in the services, I am now glad that it happened. I was, though, tired of the discipline, the lack of real freedom, and above all I missed the girls and the bright lights of London. On my regular visits home, I found myself more and more reluctant to return to the flatness and monotony of Oakington.

A few weeks before I was due to leave, the CO called me into the drawing room for a chat and tried to persuade me to sign on for a few more years. He was flattering and made my future with him appear like a garden of roses. My mind, however, was made up. He accepted my reasons, and I spent the final week there showing my successor the ropes.

I don't believe that I ever remotely considered domestic service when I returned home; in fact, history repeated itself. I found a job at Soper's in Harrow, a department store, though not selling goods of the quality I had been accustomed to at Simpson's. Now I was first salesman in the men's wear under a Mr Coe, who had himself been trained at Simpson's.

Things went smoothly but life was dull. It would have been duller still if I hadn't met and courted a girl in haberdashery. All seemed to be going well until one evening, just as we were closing, in came a customer looking for underwear for her husband. I could tell instantly by her manner that she was the awkward type.

'What size does he take?' I asked.

'I'm not quite sure.'

'Well, what sort of build is he?'

'About the same as you, only a bit bigger.'

I got out what I thought was required.

She fingered it. 'Oh, he'll want something warmer than that.'

I produced it.

She surveyed it and then looked at me, eyeing me up and down. 'No, I think it will have to be another size up.'

As I was getting what I thought she wanted, my girlfriend, who had been hovering, hissed that she was sick and tired of waiting, that we had missed the beginning of the film and that she might see me again, sometime, in the kind of voice that intimated that if she ever saw me again it would be too soon. Then to cap everything, as I produced the next size up, my customer said that she couldn't make up her mind, and that she would bring her husband in the following day so that he could make up his mind.

I'd made up mine. 'Madam,' I said, 'you can bring the King of England in tomorrow, but you won't find me here. Good night.' And having almost pushed her off the premises I decided that never again would I serve behind a counter.

My next job was with Broads of Paddington, a builders' merchant which dealt in toilets and lavatory systems. Again I was upgraded, to senior sales clerk. Despite the nature of our goods, I enjoyed the job. The work seemed easy enough; in fact it became so routine that I thought I could do it blindfold. I couldn't. I had been there about four months when the sales manager called me into his office.

'You have made a gross error on your order sheet, Russell, and caused us to lose a very fruitful source of income. As if this was not bad enough, you have made us the laughing stock of our competitors.'

It transpired that I had put the wrong numbers on many of the orders, but the one that hurt the most was that from a convent which was being renovated and had ordered six new lavatory systems. Because of my 'incompetence' they had received six urinals instead. The nuns weren't pleased, neither was the mother superior, neither was the sales manager, but our competitors, who somehow had got to hear the story, loved it and were dining out with potential customers at our expense.

'There's nothing else for it, Russell. You will have to leave immediately,' and he handed me my cards and a week's wages. I can't remember being in any way upset, but I suppose I ought to have been: it seemed as if I couldn't hold down a job. In those days they weren't hard to come by though, and since I had saved while I had been working, I thought I would take it easy for a while before deciding where my future lay. I became a drop-out of the fifties, but not for long.

I took the opportunity of freedom to get up to date with the current West End successes, hoping that by being around the theatres an opportunity to work in one might come my way. One afternoon I went to a matinee. I can't remember the name of the play, but a butler played a sizable part in it. It brought back my days with the Ramsey Raes. That evening, as I pondered over what I should do, I remembered that I had enjoyed being a butler: it offered opportunities for brushing shoulders with the upper crust and, if the play was anything to go by, a butler could be a position of some authority and influence, as well as providing the opportunity for a deal of fun both with the gentry and in the servants' quarters. I was also sure that the modern view of any kind of domestic service probably meant that there were more jobs than people to fill them.

My mind made up, I went to an agency I had heard of, Town and Country, near Sloane Square. I stopped outside and read the various cards which advertised jobs and saw one which, in my present mood, I thought would suit me well. I stepped inside and was greeted by a charming middle-aged woman. Whether that card was just a come-on or not, I'll never know, but I was told that the job was filled.

'There's no shortage of positions, though, if your qualifications are right, so I suggest you fill in this form.'

I did my best.

She glanced at it. 'Yes, your experience in the RAF will stand you in good stead. So will your hobby, which I see is acting, though I shan't tell any potential employer about it.' Her eyes twinkled. 'As a matter of fact, Lord Plunket requires a butler for his house in West Malling. Would you consider applying for that and going for an interview? He's deputy master of the Queen's household, you know.'

I think I grew two inches. 'Not in the least. I might well be interested,' I replied as if I were doing his Lordship a favour.

I had shrunk back to size again when I went to meet Lord Plunket, very nervous indeed I was. He was charm itself and quickly put me at my ease. He seemed impressed at my service experience, he liked my turnout (I'd gone to some pains over this and wore a dark blue suit, pale blue shirt and a striped tie). He asked me to walk round the room a couple of times and seemed to think I was a good mover, but then added that the position might be too quiet for me. He was often away and, though his brother Sean Plunket also lived there, there was not a lot to do. I left him with the feeling that even if I didn't get the job, I would welcome the opportunity of working for people like him, those with grace and charm. As it happened, I wasn't successful, but it soon turned out that the interview had been well worthwhile.

About a week later, Mum and I were sitting having our evening tea when there was a banging at the back door. It was Ma Hawkings whose phone number I had given for any messages.

'Kensington Palace is on the phone for you, Pete,' she announced, and from the way she said it she obviously thought it was some cinema or music hall.

I dashed into her house. There was a chap called Bysouth at the other end. He told me he was butler to HRH the Duchess of Kent, that there was a vacancy at Kensington Palace for an under-butler, that my name had been suggested by Lord Plunket, and that if I was interested would I please report for interview the following day. He also told me how to get there, and which door I should use.

I obeyed his instructions to the letter. He was pleased that I was on time as the Duchess insisted on punctuality. He then led the way to a small office off the butler's pantry. We sat looking at each other for several seconds. My first impression was that he was a member of the aristocracy himself. He was wearing a black tail coat, stiff collar, black tie, white shirt and striped trousers. Across his waistcoat, which seemed to accentuate his portly stomach, hung a gold chain. It struck me as being like a suspension bridge. I later found that one end harboured a gold watch, which he continually consulted to satisfy Her Royal Highness's insistence on time-keeping. On the other, strung like keys on a ring, was a bunch of gold sovereigns. 'You never know when they might come in handy,' he confided darkly. He had grey hair and was slightly balding. I imagined his age was around fifty-five though he never mentioned it. His voice belied his years. It was as clear and resonant as a bell, and would have reached the farthest seats in the gallery at Drury Lane.

He coughed slightly, as though to attract my attention, and the interview began. Before long I could sense that it was only a matter of form since Lord Plunket had given me his seal of approval. He ended by saying, 'Well, Peter, your service experience has been sound and I consider you will be eminently trainable.' I was delighted and rose to my feet to make an exit. 'There's just one more person who will have to interview you. Her Royal Highness's private secretary, Mr Philip Hay' (he was later knighted). Gawd, I thought, who are they appointing to what? First Plunket, then Bysouth and now Hay. All for someone to work under the butler on £225 a year.

If I had ever had any doubts about the importance of private secretaries, they were soon dispelled when Bysouth showed me into Mr Hay's office a couple of days later. It was delightfully and tastefully furnished, and would have done justice to the chairman of one of our nationalized industries. Like Lord Plunket, he quickly put me at my ease. He was tall and stately, and his face reminded me of the Duke of Windsor.

'I've heard a lot about you, Peter, both from Lord Plunket and Bysouth, who seems to think you are admirably suited for the position. All that remains now is for me to check on your past character, so I'll want the names of referees.' He explained what he meant when he saw that to me a referee was someone with a whistle. 'And I'd like to see any documents you can produce about your service life.'

Fortunately I had these with me, and I gave the local vicar's, doctor's and headmaster's names for him to write to. He seemed satisfied with what Group Captain Rae had written about me and said he saw no reason why I shouldn't start as soon as possible. I suggested the following week, and he seemed to think that would be all right. 'I'll let you know through Bysouth. He'll phone you.'

So it looked as if yours truly had got the job, but I wasn't counting my chickens. I didn't have to wait long, though: Bysouth was on the phone the following day confirming my appointment and bidding me start on the date I had suggested. Mum, it appeared, had anticipated my success, and a bottle of VP sherry was produced, of which Ma Hawkings drank the largest portion and returned home treating the neighbours to her raucous singing of 'God Save the Queen'. The following Monday found me at the back door of Kensington Palace, clutching a brand new suitcase, to begin my years of royal service.

TWO

In the few days remaining between Mr Bysouth's phone call and my joining the Duchess's household, I thought it would be as well if I got to know something about butlers, so I went to our local library. Although I found a helpful assistant, she was unable to come up with much. Little had been written about servants at that time. However, to my astonishment, I did discover that the butler's office had existed for centuries. It wasn't, as I had thought, something that had come about in Queen Victoria's reign. I learned that the French exported butlers to Britain with William the Conqueror and at the time it was a very high office. The butler was in sole charge of the wine for a large landowner, who, with his court and his army, consumed gallons of the stuff in various strengths and vintages. So, the French being the French and most choosy over their wines, and as there were few landowners, it was only natural that the butler was way up among the senior courtiers.

The same thing happened in Britain. Wine at that time was the most popular drink, even with the poor. Gradually, over the years, as the larger estates split into smaller units, the butler's office declined in importance. He still dealt with wines and liquors, but also took over the running of the household servants and thereby came to be regarded as one of the servants himself, albeit an important member of the staff.

There is, of course, a lot more to it than that and one day
some historian will uncover a wealth of detail. At the time,
however, my library visit gave me a useful insight into my
inheritance in the years that lay ahead.

By 1955, even in the most gracious of houses, the work and
the authority of the butler had waned; so, therefore, had the
importance of the under-butler, as I was to discover.

Bysouth met me the moment I was admitted to Kensington
Palace. He was a bit more master-to-man than when I had
gone for my interview, but I had anticipated that change of
attitude. He began, as it were, with the good news, and took
me to my room in the basement. It was indeed beyond my
expectations, large and opulent-looking, with heavy, red
velvet curtains and pelmets matching the red coverlet on the
bed. When Bysouth's back was turned, I gave the bed the
once-over; it was firm and well sprung. There was a walk-in
wardrobe, a Victorian chest of drawers and although the
floor was covered with blue lino, there were two or three
rugs. The room was centrally heated, so it promised to be
warmer than mine at home.

There was a large framed photograph of the Duke of
Windsor over my bed, which struck me as being a bit out of
place. Eventually I was able to change it for one of George VI
– he was after all the King I had seen and who had behaved so
admirably towards us in London during the war. Later, when
the Duchess visited my room for the one and only time, she
remarked on the change of photograph and wanted to know
why. 'It seemed more appropriate, your Royal Highness,' I
replied. She smiled slightly but made no further comment.

Having shown me my room, Bysouth left. 'Smarten yourself up, lad, and I'll take you in to introduce you to Her Royal
Highness.' I did as I was told, unpacked, put out the one or
two personal possessions I had brought with me, and then
found my way back to the butler's office. He grunted as
though in approval when he saw me, and together we went to
the drawing room where Her Royal Highness was sitting.

It was a strange meeting. Bysouth introduced me as Peter, the new member of staff.

'Ah, yes, I've been told about you, Peter,' she said, inclining her head. 'Where were you in service before?'

You can't have been told much, otherwise you'd know this was my first job, I thought.

'I had some experience in the RAF during my National Service, your Royal Highness.'

'Ah, yes, the Royal Air Force. Well I hope you'll soon get accustomed to our little ways. Mr Bysouth will tell you what they are, won't you, Bysouth?'

'Yes, your Royal Highness.'

'Ah, have you seen your quarters?'

'Yes, your Royal Highness.'

'And do you think you will be comfortable?'

'Yes, your Royal Highness.'

'Ah, well, I think that's all, Bysouth.' Then she glanced at me. 'Good morning to you, Peter.'

'Good morning, your Royal Highness.'

Not the most exhilarating or informative meeting, and when I phoned Mum later that evening, and she asked what the Duchess was like, all I could say was, 'Very beautiful.'

'Yes, but what is she really like as a person?' Mum persisted.

'I don't know now, and I'm not sure I shall ever know,' was all I could truthfully say.

I was, of course, partially wrong, but to say that I ever knew the Duchess well would be a lie. There were very few of her friends or acquaintances who could have boasted that they did. It was as if she had an inner self which was hidden from all but the few. As far as I was able to discover, she had two other selves, both very distinct; her sophisticated party manner and her almost home-spun manner, which she relaxed into whenever possible. Her occasional awkwardness has been attributed by others to shyness. I'm not sure how far I can go along with this. It is used as an excuse by and about people in many walks of life. There is also a wide-spread belief that until Marina married George, she led a precarious, sometimes wretched existence. The accent has been on revolutions, political skulduggery and the assassination of relatives (these were in fact distant relations), and there has been an attempt to argue that this had a marked effect on her character and gave her an early neurosis from which she never recovered. But every family has its ups and downs and tragedies, yet we don't all end up with a permanent mental twitch. So, as soon as I realized that I was going to stay in the Duchess's service, I made time to find out about her life, partly through talking to the servants, but mainly through books, in an attempt to get some insight into her character.

Now, I've never been one to get anything from those Bible passages where so-and-so begat so-and-so ad infinitum. Not like a pal of mine, Charlie Small, who had our Sunday school in fits when, to our teacher's consternation and embarrassment, he asked her what it was to 'begat'. She stumbled and mumbled while we kids squirmed in our seats at her discomfiture. Youth doesn't change. For those interested in Marina and Greek royal history, there is plenty of material available, but most of it doesn't really concern my story.

Marina's father, Prince Nicholas of Greece, married Helen, a relation of the Tsars of Russia. Marina was the youngest of three daughters. Like her sisters, she had a peasant for a wet nurse and later an English nanny, Miss Fox, or 'Foxy' as she was called by the children. Foxy was trained at Norland School, as were most nannies in royal households, which meant that their charges were given tough treatment (perhaps Spartan would be a more appropriate description for this Greek princess). Norland School, deep in rural Berkshire, 'exported' strict, traditional nannies all over the world. The trainees were almost always working class and the post-war scarcity of nannies greatly increased the power and status of the nursery rulers.

Marina had been born with a twisted left foot, which, although it received much treatment, meant that her left leg was always weaker and shorter than her right. She always had to wear shoes of a different size. Her parents took more interest in their children than was usual in royal households, often playing with them for hours; but they were strict disciplinarians, and many a stroke was delivered on to the princesses' backsides by their father. He used a copy of *The Times*, which, as he said, made them feel disciplined but didn't hurt. Marina was the main recipient of this punishment, as she was always the naughtiest. Foxy wasn't so considerate as Marina's father, and used her hand to administer more frequent punishments, yet the children loved her and she stayed half a century in service with the family. I got on well with her, perhaps because she had grown older and softer by the time we met. She told me that my Princess at the age of three was rather wilful, wanted her own way and was prepared to scream her head off to get it. My experience of the Princess showed me how wrong one can be trying to trace back later traits of character to early childhood.

The Princess's first visit to England was when she was four. Her mother and father stayed with Edward VII at Buckingham Palace, as well as touring around the houses of friends that the prince had made when he was a young man. The three princesses and Foxy enjoyed themselves on the beaches at Bognor and Westgate-on-Sea.

They also visited Russia twice a year. I liked the description of a state banquet which Marina attended in 1914 when she was seven. In the great banqueting hall, which extended the whole width of the palace, 3000 guests could sit and dine. Countless courses were served on gold plates, with each royal guest looked after by a court official. The wine was first poured out by a footman, who handed it to a page to taste, and it was then served to the guests. They took no chances in the Tsar's court. The doorway on these occasions was guarded by six coal-black Negroes in native dress, armed with gleaming scimitars. They were a present to the Tsar from the Emperor of Abyssinia.

During this holiday in Russia, the little girls sailed in the royal yacht from Sebastopol to Athens and back. At Sebastopol they were taken on the royal train with salons upholstered in silks and damasks, and they were nearly up to their knees in Turkish carpets. They slept in real beds with sheets of fine linen and a silk eiderdown. At each station where they stopped, they were given sweets, chocolates and fruit. Foxy didn't have too bad a time of it either. She wrote home: 'My nurseries consist of eight or ten beautifully furnished rooms; a dining room, two salons, anterooms, night nursery, dressing room and bathroom.' However, Foxy came in for some criticism from the Grand Duchess when she opened the bedroom windows and let in the bitter freezing air. Later, when she had cause to spank the princesses the Duchess complained to their mother, 'That dreadful woman knocks them about.'

I'm afraid I've got a bit ahead of myself. Princess Marina's life was somewhat interrupted by the outbreak of the first Balkan war in 1912. She went to Paris and later to Russia. In Paris they stayed at the Hotel Continental, reckoned to be the grandest hotel there at the time. The war didn't last long, the Greek army acquitted itself well and Marina was back with her family after only six months' absence. Six very enjoyable months, I would have thought, for a child to have spent.

Shortly after her return, her granddad, King George I of Greece, was assassinated. He was sixty-eight. It must have been a shock, but still, granddads do die and he had reached a fair age, and I can't believe it had a lasting effect on her.

Then came the Great War. Since King Constantine, who succeeded George I, insisted that Greece remained neutral, Princess Marina was spared all the horrors that children of other monarchs had to endure, no matter which side they were on. Constantine's insistence on neutrality may have been due to his German-born wife; on the other hand, there were many, including our own Queen Mary, who had roots in Germany. Not for nothing was it called the Stud Farm of Kings. The nearest Marina came to the war was when French warships bombarded Athens, but again history tells us that she and her sisters found this great fun, watching from their nursery window, and were furious when their mother discovered them and insisted that they went down to the cellars. In 1917 King Constantine was deposed and Marina and her family took refuge in Switzerland. They stayed in a hotel and were joined by other members of the clan. Then the Russian revolution began, culminating in 1918 with the assassination of the Tsar. But the Grand Duchess escaped to Paris, taking with her a sizable amount of her jewels, which meant that she and her nearest and dearest would never have to want for the readies. When she died in 1920, a goodly portion of them went to Marina's father. Around Christmas 1920, Constantine was restored to the throne and Prince and Princess Nicholas and the girls went back to Greece. There too went Foxy, who had been advised by the British embassy to leave the family at the outbreak of war.

Unfortunately for Constantine and the others, the Greece he returned to was in the grip of war fever. Its people wanted to fight the Turks to establish their sovereignty over Asia Minor. From the beginning they stood little chance, and the war ended in September 1922 with total defeat. The princesses were not much affected as their mama took them off to Paris in the spring of 1922. Their father escaped to Italy and they were reunited at Palermo. Again, they were lucky: the princesses' money and jewellery were smuggled out and returned to them. Somehow, I think that all this to-ing and fro-ing was the only thing that Bysouth learned about the family, and it was this that made him collect the gold sovereigns which he held in the pocket opposite his gold watch.

Once again the Princess and her sisters visited England. The princesses, Olga and Elizabeth, had a joint coming-out and it was hoped, even in the highest British circles, that one of Queen Mary's sons, the Prince of Wales in particular, might choose a bride from one of them. In fact only Princess Olga returned with a prize, the twenty-nine-year-old Prince Paul of Yugoslavia. They were married in October 1923. The rest of the family now lived in Paris, though they spent some time in the South of France. They've been described as being very poor, though how apt this description is can be assessed from the fact that they kept four servants and had a car and a chauffeur. Princess Nicholas sold her tiara to Queen Mary and I'm sure the money that passed hands wasn't just hay. The family also rented their house in Athens to the Grand Bretange, Athens' biggest and smartest hotel, and Prince Nicholas, who was an accomplished artist, sold many of his paintings for good money. Both Princess Marina and Princess Elizabeth were dressed by the French couturier, Jean Patou. So, for my money, if that is what is considered as being poor, even comparatively speaking, there was no hardship; yet Marina's biographers weep crocodile tears over her situation at that time. Indeed, in her later years when she was in Britain, the Princess was to know worse financial troubles.

She completed her education at a finishing school in Paris, concentrating particularly on art. She was a cinema buff, going at least once a week, and she loved the chocolates and the splendid pastries and gateaux that the French do so well. She travelled around Europe and spent a lot of time with her sister Olga in Yugoslavia. It was on a visit with her to England that she first met Prince George, the youngest surviving son of our royal family. Later, in Prince Paul's 'White Palace' in Yugoslavia, he proposed to her. She was then twenty-eight years old.

Now looking back over her early years, I think it must be admitted that Marina didn't have too bad a time. She had repeated glimpses of glories that are now legendary, the love and attention of her parents, the fun of life with her sisters. She saw some adventure and heard first hand of the adventures of others. She travelled widely over Europe in great comfort. She had the best of everything that was going, and, above all, her immediate family remained intact. I think there must be 999 girls out of a thousand who would have been only too happy to have changed places with her.

But back to mundane me before I complete the Marina saga. No sooner had Bysouth and I left the drawing room than he started my indoctrination. 'You had better meet the staff, though you won't get to know them all well since they leave at the drop of a hat. In any case, many of them are laid off when we go to Coppins, so that we never see them again. I'm afraid things aren't what they used to be,' he added with a smile. (Coppins was the family's country house, near Iver in Buckinghamshire; it was mainly used in the late spring and summer.)

We made our way to the servants' hall. I didn't meet all the staff at once, but it consisted of butler, head housemaid, two lady's maids – one for Marina and the other for her daughter, Princess Alexandra – and three housemaids. There was also someone called an odd-man. I had always thought an odd man was either a chap who was slightly batty or one who came to a party without a girlfriend, but in a household like this he was the person who did all the heavy work, carrying coal and logs, humping trunks and suitcases, as well as being given any task that nobody else wanted to do. There were also two chauffeurs for the three cars – Marina's Rolls, a Humber Pullman and a shooting brake.

Mr Bysouth was right. I never did get to know any members of the staff and could only put a name to the few that came with us to Coppins. After the war there had been something of a shift in attitude towards domestic work and this, coupled with prosperity in the 1950s and an abundance of jobs, meant that servants were harder to come by and less willing to stay for low wages, even in such grand households.

We did, however, achieve some semblance of the old days when we ate. The table would be set and places taken in order of seniority, with Princess Marina's lady's maid at the top, Alexandra's maid on her left, and the head housemaid on her right. The junior housemaids sat in the middle, as did the kitchen maid. I took my place at the bottom of the table, opposite Marina's lady's maid, with the odd-man on my right. He kept bobbing up and down, for it was his responsibility to serve the food. The chauffeurs never ate with us: they were given money to have their meals out, but they scrounged what they could from the kitchen.

Bysouth was never present on these occasions. He would take his lunch and tea with his wife in the butler's pantry. He prepared the meal himself, on a small methylated spirit stove on which he would heat a pan of water. Into this he would put two eggs to be boiled for exactly three and a half minutes. Meantime he would butter two slices of bread and cut them into narrow strips – 'soldiers' as Mum and I called them. These he would dunk in the eggs, thereby only eating the yolk and a little of the white. He tried to play it secretly, but all the staff knew of his quaint habit. He had his evening meal at home, for he and his wife were given a furnished flat in London and a small house at Iver.

We boasted a staff sitting room in the basement of the palace. It was comfortably furnished, with a settee and a couple of chintz-covered easy chairs. There were also chintz curtains and cushions. It was a charming place in which to entertain our friends and relations. Once, when Mum came, the head housemaid was changing some curtains in the Princess's boudoir. They were thought to be getting a bit old and she offered them to Mum, who accepted them with alacrity. I don't think there was anyone in our street who hadn't had a sight of them by the time Mum hung them.

For better or for worse, the vast majority of people treat royalty as though they were some form of deity. There was a tale told in servants' halls concerning the time Queen Mary went to one of London's theatres that hadn't a royal box with a royal loo. Alternative arrangements were made with an

Elsan. The following morning, while the chars were cleaning the front of the house, the manager made his round. Finding that the royal facility hadn't been used, he decided to christen it himself. Half an hour later, as the chars were leaving, they waved some little bottles at him, displaying them with great glee. 'We may not have seen Her Majesty but we've got something of hers to remember her by,' one shouted jubilantly. The manager didn't have the heart to disillusion them. That, he thought, accounts for the expression, 'the Royal We'.

On my first day Bysouth took me on a tour of the house, starting at the main entrance. There was a large porch, supported by four pillars. Three steps led up to the black double-fronted door. This opened onto a marble-floored hall; another two steps and a turning to the right gave onto what was called the gallery. In fact, it was a corridor with tapestries on either side, about sixteen feet wide and thirty-five feet long, with a square hall at the end. Under foot was a multi-patterned Indian or Turkish carpet on a parquet floor. Along the sides of the gallery were small antique tables with marble tops, decorated with pieces of jade. They were interspersed with gilt chairs with deep red upholstery. These merely added to the overall appearance of the gallery; I never saw anyone sit on them, except the occasional housemaid taking a rest and she quickly moved if she heard anyone coming. Resting was frowned on both by family and senior servants. In Marina's opinion the chairs were not there for the use of menial bottoms.

The gallery led to the main hall. This was dominated by an oil painting of Princess Nicholas, Marina's mother. It was all of four feet wide and eight feet long. Whatever its artistic merits, it was a perfect likeness; I met the Greek princess a number of times during my stay with Marina. In the picture she was dressed in black, her hair was short and she had a slight smile, though her eyes were dark and sad. It could have been a portrait of Marina herself, so much did she resemble her mother. Above the picture was a strip light which had to be switched on at night. If it wasn't, Bysouth would receive a rocket, which grew more powerful as it was passed down to me, the odd-man or one of the housemaids.

In the middle of the hall was a large mahogany table with a vase in the centre. What period it was or where it came from, I never found out, though it's my opinion that it had once graced the Tsar's palace. It was probably a present from Sir Harold and Lady Zia Wernher, who were close friends.

The parquet floor was scattered with antique rugs, much to the annoyance of the housemaids who had both to polish the floors and to clean the rugs daily. 'Double the bleeding work, for the same amount of bleeding money,' they grumbled.

Whenever there were guests, the hall was decorated with the Duke's collection of snuffboxes, which the visitors gasped over. They were mounted in a case on the table, to be seen but not touched – not touched, that is, by anyone but Bysouth and myself. I once counted them but forget now how many there were – scores anyway. Some were silver, but most were gilt and needed careful handling when we cleaned them.

Leading from the hall there were three rooms: the dining room, the private secretary's room, young Prince Edward's study. He was then about twenty and with his regiment. It was a small room, with a desk, a number of his father's books and a few of his own, family photos and magazines, mostly about cars. He was very keen on driving, I think he still is, despite a couple of near disasters when he was young. He would often entertain one or two of his cronies in his study.

The dining room was functional. Normally the table was kept so that it could seat eight, but extensions could be added to seat four more at a time, up to twenty-four places. There were sideboards on either side, from which the food was served from electric hot plates. There were a few pictures around the walls and, at the far end, two alcoves with fitted glass doors in which was displayed the Princess's valuable china.

At the end of the hall, next to the main staircase, was a short corridor leading to the drawing room. It was here the grog tray was kept, which Bysouth or I had to maintain twice a day at about 11.30 in the morning and again in the afternoon when we had finished setting up for dinner. We had to see there was ice, lemon, a selection of nuts, stuffed olives and whatever else was in fashion at the time. There were four large glass decanters for gin, whisky, brandy and dry sherry. The Princess drank rarely, but some of her guests had unsteady hands, particularly those from the Russian court. Strangely, they didn't drink vodka; it seems they had acquired a taste for whisky and, unlike Oliver Twist, they didn't ask for more, they just took it. The drawing room was distinctively feminine, a large room, looking out onto a walled garden with a lawn, a couple of small trees and some attractive borders. The room had a fitted green carpet and heavy velvet curtains to match in the eight windows that flanked each side. The walls were cream and were hung with portraits, including two of the Princess's own pictures. Like most well-born girls of her generation, she had been taught to paint.

The fireplace was of the Adam period, and had been put in when the Princess moved there. There were the inevitable clocks, a gold French one dominating the mantelpiece. I say inevitable because the Duke of Kent had collected clocks; when he was alive there were at least three in every room at Coppins, I believe. My predecessor, I suppose, must have had the job of winding them. Now that staff were thinner on the ground, Bysouth took over the task.

The furniture was light, more chintz, though two of the couches were plain, one green and the other brown, blending in with the overall colour of the room. There were two large four-seater settees, angled towards the fireplace, several three- or four-legged sidetables, one of them with a cabinet containing the games Marina liked to play. Her favourite was Scrabble.

There was a large coffee table with ashtrays, silver cigarette boxes and matchbox holders. Whenever convenient, Bysouth or I would take these boxes and half withdraw a match so that the head pointed outwards. The Princess could then light her cigarettes without distracting her attention from whoever she was speaking to. The room was lit mainly by side lamps with cream or cream and green shades. An immediate and surprising experience on entering the room was the sweet aroma, which came from some substance placed on the electric light bulbs to give the whole room a distinctive smell.

Off the drawing room was the Princess's boudoir, which was, I felt, the cosiest room in the house. It was small, bright and intimate. The walls were papered in a glowing crimson material. Around the room were the miniatures which the Princess had collected, both in England and on her travels. An important item was her desk, a beautiful Queen Anne piece, where she would sit in the mornings writing letters, and on which stood photos of her husband and the children at various ages.

The staircase, which was the main feature of the hall, was deep-carpeted in blue, each step held in position by thick brass rods, which, attractive though they were, must have been cursed by generations of housemaids whose job it had been to polish them. I don't know whether the staircase itself was period or not. When I first saw it, I thought, that's from *Sunset Boulevard*, and I had a vision of Gloria Swanson gliding down it. I had the same sensation, only more so, when I first saw Princess Marina, dressed to kill and ready for the opera or theatre, with her glorious face surmounted by a glistening tiara, her gloved fingers barely touching the balustrade, stopping some few steps from the hall, straightening her shoulders and posing, for she knew that her staff loved to see her on such occasions. It was for this vision, after all, that we worked so hard, and my God were we proud of her. None, I suppose, more than Miss Arter, Marina's lady's maid, who, somewhat selfishly we thought, looked on her as her own creation.

But to return to earth. On the walls of the stairwell were oil paintings of dignitaries, some ugly looking, obviously of British stock, whom I didn't recognize and had no desire to get to know. Left at the top of the stairs was Princess Marina's bedroom suite. It was bright, with white walls, crimson carpets, chintz curtains and covers, and white and gilt furniture. It suited the Princess's character. Her hairdresser, René, would often remark that it was like going into the apartment of the most glamorous of film stars; he should have known because he was probably the most fashionable hairdresser of the day. Marina owed him a lot because he matched her hairdos to the hats for which she was so famous. To give her her due, she acknowledged the debt whenever praise was heaped on her.

Leaving Marina's rooms and passing the staircase on the right, we came to Prince Edward's bedroom and bathroom. It was a man's room, dark blue carpets, curtains and bedspread, with a blue bathroom suite, royal blue I suppose you'd call it. On his dressing table was a photograph of his father and mother. His ivory hairbrushes were initialled 'G' and had belonged to his father. His fitted wardrobe contained both civilian and military clothes, of which there was quite a quantity.

Next to Prince Edward's room was Alexandra's, all pink and bright. It was as big as her brother's, as feminine as his was masculine. The furry toys scattered over her bed showed that she was still a young light-hearted girl and she behaved, like one.

There was a corridor on the left which led to Prince Michael's bedroom. He had just gone to Eton when I joined. When he was at home his room was typical of any young boy's: clothes left where they had been taken off and all sorts of odds and ends scattered around the place. Although the boys added life and vitality to the palace, I wasn't sorry when their holidays ended.

Along the passage from Prince Michael's room was the bathroom, two guest rooms and Miss Arter's room, with a workroom next door and another at the end of the corridor. The second or attic floor was reached only by the back stairs, which were those used by the servants. There were three staff bedrooms for the housemaids and Alexandra's lady's maid, two bathrooms and a lumber room housing trunks, suitcases and a multitude of hat boxes, apart from other bits and pieces. Next to it was a washing and workroom for the smalls, all the main laundry being sent out.

One other room in the attic fascinated me: there the old toys were kept, those that the children had been given when they were younger but which they had now grown out of. It was like Hamley's of ten to fifteen years back. Some of these toys would be taken to orphanages, but others remained. There were dolls and dolls houses, pedal bikes and tricycles, a rocking horse and every sort of mechanical toy; forts and lead soldiers, most without heads which were replaced by matchsticks instead, and a complete train layout mounted on a board with which I passed many a snatched and secret hour. I was caught one day by Prince Michael, who thought it a huge joke. I swore him to secrecy, but he used it as a kind of blackmail whenever he wanted something which I knew he wasn't permitted.

Down now to the basement, where my bedroom and the staff sitting room were. Here there was also a spare room, the odd-man Bernard's room, Bysouth's office, a place for storing spare furniture, and something we called the cement room, where the spare china was kept. It was christened that because it was undecorated and there were no windows. It was a place into which I often tried to inveigle an attractive housemaid, alas never successfully. Princess Marina also stored the staff Christmas presents there. She chose them herself and always wrapped them too. However, it was common practice for the staff, when they saw their presents in there, to unwrap them carefully and take a peep.

Fortunately for me, one Christmas the odd-man wasn't quick enough and when I saw that our presents had been added, I took a quick look at mine and found a tie which was not my style at all. So I opened the odd-man's parcel. He'd got a very nice pullover. I tried it on and it fitted me a treat. It was easy for me to convince myself that it was much too small for him, so I packed both presents up again and swopped the labels. The odd-man was not exactly pleased to get the tie; in fact he went on for days about it, but then he was never satisfied. The following Christmas he got a scarf. 'What bloody good is that to me? I've got one already,' he grumbled.

I was able to make it up to him that time.

'How much do you want for it?' I asked. 'Would a couple of quid do?'

'I'd be very satisfied with that.'

'I'll tell you what I'll do,' I said. 'I'll take it down our street and see if I can flog it.'

We agreed and I had no difficulty getting the price. For once he was happy and offered me five bob for my pains, but that pullover was still on my conscience so I refused it. Quite the little hero I was in his eyes for a day or two.

Sensibly the kitchen quarters were on the ground floor. Off the pantry was the silver safe, where I was to spend many an hour cursing the fact that silver tarnishes even if it hasn't been used, and Bysouth for his insistence that it should bear the most searching inspection. It was ten times harder than polishing buttons in the RAF and Bysouth had the piercing eyes of a sergeant major. Such, however, is the way of the world that when I became a butler, with a full staff, I was similarly demanding of those under me. For the uninitiated, apart from being a cleaning room, the silver safe contains not only the tableware, but also the cups, trophies, orders and in the Princess's case, the snuffboxes, many of her most precious jade pieces and much of her jewellery which was not in frequent use.

That then was Kensington Palace as I first knew it. Perhaps

I should mention that as next-door neighbours in the Clock House lived the Earl and Countess of Athlone.

No sooner had we completed my tour of inspection, than Bysouth waded in on my duties. Since we were not over-staffed, we shared some chores with the housemaids, and as there were no valets, when the boys were on holiday I was lumbered with the work that would have been theirs. By the time Bysouth had finished outlining the job, I saw myself as some sort of galley slave, with him, the Princess and the two boys ready to lash me with whips should I falter.

However, as I discovered, it was like my other job. A little experience went a long way and, while practice may not have made it perfect, I believe I was able to give some sort of continuity in my service when other staff were leaving, and to maintain a degree of satisfaction from my employers, though you are never given full appreciation until after you have left. Then you hear second-hand remarks like, 'Now, when Peter was here he always did so and so' or 'Peter would never have dreamed of allowing that.' I'm not being conceited by saying this, as I've heard it said about so many others.

THREE

At Kensington Palace my day started at 6.30. I dressed quickly, made myself a cup of tea and then supervised the breakfast trays. If we had guests, the breakfasts would be taken to their rooms and received by their valets or lady's maids. In Marina's case, Miss Arter was outside her door ready to take the tray. Meantime, the odd-man had prepared our breakfasts. I would then go through the ground floor, collecting any glasses and ashtrays that needed washing. I would also check the desks for notepaper and envelopes, fill the cigarette boxes, often at the same time helping myself to a couple by way of perks, and arrange the matchboxes. I would also inspect the fire to make sure it was burning well and the grate was clean. It was the under-housemaid's job to polish the grate and the surround, and since it was the old-fashioned type, it required black-leading. This, though it gives a uniquely beautiful sheen, is a filthy and degrading job for anyone to have to do.

If either or both of the Princes were in residence, it was I who had to attend to them. I called them and I would ask what they were going to wear, suit or casual. When I had managed to wake them into consciousness, they would, between curses, give me some sort of answer. I would then run the baths, drape the towels over the chairs and lay bathmats, unscrew the toothpaste and take the bottle caps off after-

shave lotion and hair oil. While they were bathing, I would
lay out their clothes and for Edward would allow for a choice
from two shirts and three ties. I would change their pockets,
again generally nicking one of Edward's cigarettes as I went
through them. In the meantime both of them had become
more genial and chatty.

My other duties had to dovetail in with taking care of the
princes when they were home. They were a pleasure to look
after, so I didn't mind the extra work. Bysouth would do
more, so would the odd-man, and I think we can justifiably
say that things generally went without a hitch, and with few
rough words exchanged between us.

After all the breakfast things had been cleared, I would
repair to the silver safe. The cleaning was indeed hard work,
but for those who seek to achieve the wonderful results we
obtained, I'll explain how it was done. Not for us the Silvo or
similar preparations which are found in most households. We
used Goddard's powder. This was mixed with a little water in
a saucer. The pink paste was then spread on whatever item
we were cleaning. We used a cloth, but every so often we
would discard this and rub with our thumbs and fingers. It
seems that the heat thus generated had some reaction on the
silver, softening it and allowing the mixture to impregnate
the metal, giving a bluish tinge. The paste was then allowed
to dry and finally polished with a chamois leather. Silver par
excellence was the result. Once a year we would rouge it,
using a white rouge and a deal more finger and thumb action
to remove any deep scratches that might have accumulated.
No wonder in the old days you could tell an under-butler by
the state of the balls of his thumbs, for he had probably been
doing the job for countless years before being considered for
promotion.

There was a similar old-fashioned ritual for knife-
sharpening. With the invention of stainless steel, one would
have thought that the real steel knives would have gone out of
fashion, and with them those circular knife machines that

were wound round like the old-fashioned mangle. Not at the palace, they hadn't. Our machines came aptly enough from George Kent's of Luton, who also provided the necessary powder. This was shaken into various holes, the blades were inserted and, as the machine revolved, the knives were sharpened and cleaned at the same time.

We took similar pains with the glasses. We would prepare a bowl of hot soapy water; first swill the base; then, holding the stem, swish it round the bowl, shake it and run it under the hot tap (not too hot, though) to rinse it off; finally give it another slight shake, and then polish it with a linen cloth, so that when it was held up to the light you could be sure there were no marks on the glass. Many people who concern themselves with getting wine right focus their attention on the bottle, on the correct temperature and on giving the wine time to breathe. They forget that the condition of the glass is of equal, if not greater importance. The cleaning of decanters and claret jugs is also an art in itself. Both can get stained, particularly around the bottom. The way we removed these stains was by putting lead pellets (like those from a cartridge) inside with just a touch of water and shaking the receptacle vigorously so that the pellets bounced around the bottom, thus removing the stain. Drying a decanter by any normal method is not easy. Bysouth found the only way was to hold the decanter's neck between his legs and vibrate it furiously. It may have looked a bit peculiar but it did the trick.

When we used the ordinary china, the odd-man did the washing-up, but if we were entertaining and used the best, Bysouth and I would set to. It seemed unfair that the odd-man should have to carry the can if anything got broken. The sinks in the kitchens at Kensington Palace were wood-lined, thus limiting the breakages that might otherwise occur.

The same care was shown by the Princess towards her marvellous collection of ornamental china. About twice a year orders would come through that she was going to attend to it. Out would come two trestle tables, a new washing-up cloth, a sponge and a mop. There would be three or four bowls of warm water, half a dozen teacloths and two pairs of rubber gloves. When she was ready, she would walk down, carrying an apron over her left arm, with Miss Arter at her heels. Once the Princess was in position, Miss Arter would come forward and help Marina into her apron. Operations then commenced. I was standing nearby, ready to change the water. I enjoyed watching Marina at her work as I thought it brought her in touch with what went on daily below stairs, though if we had gone to the same near pageantry that she gave to the occasion, God knows when our work would have finished. This was the only household chore which Marina physically involved herself with.

Whenever any silver needed repairing or any jewellery required either cleaning or repair, it was my job to take it along to Cartier or to a silversmith. Of course, the jewellery should really have been taken by the lady's maid but she could easily have been recognized and set upon. Occasionally Miss Arter would meet me at the jeweller's if the Princess wanted some special work doing. I was always treated with the greatest respect on these visits – as if I were a high-spending customer – but I was made to feel that the pieces really belong to the craftsmen, they treated them with such reverence. They even had photographs of some of the pieces so that if they were badly damaged they would know how to repair them.

Fortunately Marina didn't drink morning coffee, though on occasions she might join her secretary in a cup if he was having one. Just before midday I would attend to the grog tray, then at twelve the staff had their lunch and at ten to one Bysouth and I would begin removing things to the hot plates in the dining room. Around that time Marina would start alerting her flock. 'It's lunch time, Ed. Are you ready? Michael, leave whatever you're doing and come down at once. Alexandra, I hope you've changed from whatever it was you were wearing this morning. It was most unbecoming and didn't suit you a bit. Come on, all of you, we don't want to keep Bysouth waiting.'

'She doesn't give a damn whether she keeps me waiting or not, it's this fetish she has on time-keeping,' Bysouth would remark. He then pulled his watch from his waistcoat and precisely on the dot of one went to the sitting room and announced: 'Lunch is ready, your Royal Highness.'

I didn't like his use of the word 'ready'. In the plays I had seen or acted in, it was 'luncheon is served' and that, I decided, was going to be my way of making the announcement.

The meal over, we cleared, the table was laid up for dinner, and I prepared the grog tray for the evening drinks. This practice I know would have been frowned on in most houses. It was thought that dust would gather on the tableware. When I mentioned this to Bysouth, he snorted. 'There's no dust in my dining room. Even if there was, I'd still do it. When would we get any time off otherwise? If I didn't see Mrs Bysouth in the afternoon, she'd think something was up, and if Mrs Bysouth thinks something's up, she's not pleasant company.'

He always referred to his wife as Mrs Bysouth. Never did I hear him mention her Christian name. He was right about the time off of course. We took it in turns to serve tea, so it meant either two or four hours' rest before we were on duty again.

During the afternoon, the phone was put through to me or, if I was off, to the head housemaid. Princess Marina always rested and wouldn't speak on the phone unless someone of higher rank was on the other end. Tea could be simple if she was on her own, just a tray in the boudoir or in the secretary's office. If there were guests, it was the full treatment. If there were children like Prince Charles or Princess Anne there, it would be in the dining room. She loved any occasion with children, sitting at the head of the table chatting away to them, treating them always as equals and that way winning their affection and confidence. There would be sandwiches,

savories prepared by our chef, specialities from Fortnum and
Mason, and cakes from a little Belgian patisserie in
Knightsbridge which the Princess used for her bread, rolls
and croissants.

An extravagance that I found fascinating was that every
day, even when we were at Coppins, the Belgian patisserie
would always deliver. The chauffeur would fetch the bread
and croissants from Iver station, a special journey just for this
tiny parcel. It is the kind of eccentricity that only royals can
indulge in. The butter, cream and cheese came from Windsor
in the same way. In London food for the household generally
came from Harrods or Fortnum and Mason, or was sent up
from the gardens at Coppins. While in residence in the country we had homegrown fruit and vegetables and were usually
supplied by the village store for routine groceries.

One thing that Marina always had by her was a box of
Floris chocolates. These were a constant temptation, both to
the housemaids and to myself. Although they disappeared
fast, Her Royal Highness never remarked upon it. She must
have known we picked at them, but presumably thought of
them as a form of recompense for good work. Of course,
there were the inevitable cigarettes; but at that time, although
I was a heavy smoker, they didn't tempt me, for they were
Greek and had what to me was a harsh, burning taste.

Dinner was the formal meal of the day whether we had
guests or not. For the first couple of months I could feel
Bysouth's eyes following every move I made, and after dinner
he would criticize my behaviour. I think I learned fairly fast,
as much to get away from his constant staring as out of
anxiety to do the job properly. As far as the Princess was
concerned, I might have always been there. She was aware
that I was learning the job, but at first she never showed it.
Later it was different. By her side she always had a notepad in
a folding silver case. There was a slim silver pencil by its side.
If anything went wrong, and this applied particularly if we
had guests, she would make a note and, as likely as not, we

would be criticized for some breach of behaviour the following day. 'Sauce with lunch too rich,' 'Coffee too strong,' 'Arter to arrange with Marks and Spencer for selection of pastel scarves to be sent on approval,' were typical comments. It was an irritating thing to have to live with, but we were not alone. I know that Lady Zia Wernher for one had the same habit, and I understand her comments on misdemeanours were more bitter and pungent than Princess Marina's.

At home the Princess was a light eater, but not because she was concerned about her figure for, according to Miss Arter, she seldom mentioned it. To my surprise, when she was alone, the Princess would often ask for a fry-up for supper — bacon, eggs, kidneys, but never chips. Two small boiled potatoes was all she wanted.

Dinner over and cleared away, what was left of the day was ours. As we had to rise early, particularly if we had guests, we were usually too tired to watch television in the staff sitting room but went straight to bed.

It was about a week after I joined that Bysouth said, 'Time for you go to the tailor, lad, get yourself properly kitted up.' I think he hadn't suggested this immediately as he wanted to be sure that I was right for the job and that I seemed likely to stay. In some quite well-known and wealthy houses male staff on joining were directed to a room where a number of secondhand footman outfits were laid out. They were made to try these on by the butler in the hope that one set fitted. Indeed, it was possible to get an early impression of what the job was going to be like from the outfits available. If there was a number of them, it meant that the staff turnover was rapid, from which could be construed that it was not a happy house to work in. There is also something demeaning about wearing secondhand clothes. I always insisted on my uniforms being made to measure.

Bysouth directed me to a tailor in Uxbridge near Iver, our summer residence. I was fitted with a day suit, one of which I could order each year, though it had to be either dark grey or navy; it was used when none of the family was in residence. For duty, a black tail coat, striped trousers and a single-breasted black waistcoat (only full butlers wore double-breasted), a black tie, five shirts and two pairs of black shoes. For evening wear I had dress tails, a flyaway collar and white tie with four stiff-fronted shirts. I had two fittings and when the clothes were finally delivered, I dressed myself up in each suit in turn and felt no end of a dog.

Some years later, though, I heard the story of the footmen who went to Robert Lillico, the tailors in Maddox Street. After Lillico had finished measuring, he would draw a foot-man to one side and whisper, 'Dear boy, you're entitled to a long pair of woollen underpants to go with each of your livery trousers. If, however, like many footmen, you don't choose to wear them, go downstairs and my brother Bob will give you something in their place.' Most elected for down-stairs, where brother Bob was cutting out the suits. They would explain their presence.

'Ah, another no-nonsense pants man. Come and sit down.' He would then take a glass and fill it with whisky from the cask on the table. 'This, dear boy, is your recompense.' If he liked the cut of your jib, he would replenish the glass, and many's the footman who has staggered back on duty to be greeted by an angry butler.

When I heard the story, I couldn't help wondering what the clothes must have been like, for Bob was the cutter, and if the footman consumed plenty, he must have drunk still more. But Lillico's are in business today with a fine reputation, so I can only assume he had an infinite capacity.

It was some time later that I was fitted for headwear. One morning Mr Bysouth interrupted my silver-cleaning to inform me that the Princess had decided to drive to Coppins to sort out some books, and wished me to go with her to help.

'Have you got a bowler hat?' he inquired.

'No,' I said. 'What on earth would I need one for?'

'Well, you can't drive in the royal car unless you have one, so get a taxi, make haste to Barkers and get fitted.'

'Let's have a look at it,' Bysouth said on my return. 'Yes, that fits all right, but we'll have no wearing of it at that jaunty angle, you're not on the boards of the Palladium now, you know. Flat on top of the head it must be, and while you're in the car, you look straight in front of you; you're not here to enjoy a view of the countryside. Now, about the hat routine. When the Rolls arrives here at the front door, you will get into it next to Freddy [the chauffeur]. When I open the door, you'll get out of the car, but to do that you'll have to take your hat off. Once out, you put it on again, but when the Princess gets near the car, you'll take it off as a mark of respect. You'll open the door for her, and I shall put the rug over her knees. You'll shut the door and put your hat on. Then you'll open the front door, but you'll have to take your hat off to get in. Once inside, back on goes your hat. Now, when you get to Coppins, you must take your hat off, open the door, get out of the car, put it on again, open her door, but take your hat off as she gets out. Do you think you've got it?'

I felt like a juggler practising a new trick, but all went well until we got to a country lane, when down went the communicating window, and the Princess told Freddy to stop. I didn't know what was happening, so I just went through the second part of the routine. I notice that she had changed her shoes for boots, her tailored town coat for a country tweed, and had taken her hat off and was wearing a headscarf.

'Thank you, very much,' was all she said, as she walked off.

I turned to Freddy. 'What the hell's going on?'

'It's all right, she's going to walk across the fields to her house.'

We arrived ahead of her to find a puzzled Alice, the head housekeeper. We waited by the car until the Princess appeared. It was a sight worth waiting for. Some years back, the Duke had planted several thousand daffodil bulbs in a field leading up to the house. The Princess had walked to the field and every so often she had stopped to pick a flower. Cradled in her arms was a sheaf of daffodils. There was something almost pathetic about her figure as she approached us. It reminded me of Wordsworth's poem about daffodils, and for once I remembered something I'd been forced to learn in school.

Perhaps now is the time to turn back the clock and for me to complete my story of the Princess's life from the time of her marriage until the Duke's untimely death in 1942. I have to go back even further to explore the upbringing of the man she married.

Prince George was born in 1902, the fourth son and fifth child of George V and Queen Mary. Although it is probable that King George will go down in history as one of the worst fathers that any son could have, Prince George got off the lightest of the children, as so often the youngest in a family does. After early lessons in the palace schoolroom, and later from a tutor, he went to a small preparatory school in Broadstairs, where he misbehaved disgracefully. On holidays, however, he was made to toe the line by his brothers, particularly by Prince Henry, later Duke of Gloucester, who was inclined to bully him. By his father's decree, whether he had a calling for the sea or not, he was sent to the Royal Naval College at Osborne, and from there went to Dartmouth.

In fact, he was a very bad sailor. He was constantly seasick, which probably led to later stomach trouble and insomnia. Apart from his naval duties, the Prince went on three tours, to Canada, South America and South Africa. Eventually, on medical advice, King George allowed him to retire from active service in the Navy and he worked at the Foreign Office and the Home Office. He didn't care for the normal social pursuits of princes, preferring to sunbathe, gamble at a casino or dance the night away on the French Riviera, rather than the more usual hunting, shooting and fishing. He also loved beautiful things, like antiques, pictures, books, the ballet and, of course, attractive women. Speed in fast cars and aeroplanes delighted him and he was fearless. He played the piano by ear and would strum the tunes of Gershwin and Cole Porter or any of the more popular light composers of the times.

So, Prince George, a mixture of courage, good looks, gaiety, moodiness and occasional insensitivity, was, in his way, a suitable husband for Marina with her three-quarters Russian blood. In the staff quarters the maxim, 'In all Russians there is a mixture of saint and sinner', was often sagely repeated.

The King was pleased with his choice of the Princess. He was fond of a pretty face and to him, and indeed to Queen Mary, it was a marriage combining convenience and romance. To the British people it was presented, as all royal weddings are, as some kind of fairy tale, and they were ready for one, for life in Britain over recent years had been dingy, with the General Strike, widespread unemployment, and unfulfilled promises. They took the couple to their hearts. Yet until his engagement in August 1934, Prince George had been the least known and the least publicized of the royals and Princess Marina had never been heard of.

Their return from Yugoslavia where the betrothal had taken place was a sensation. 'England gave Princess Marina such a burst of welcome as has not been equalled since the day Alexandra came across the seas from Denmark seventy-two years ago' was the opinion of the *Daily Express*.

From now until the wedding day, all was bustle and go, with the Princess being constantly mobbed by crowds whenever she appeared in public. On 20 November 1934, nine days before the wedding, the King created Prince George, who up to then had been his only untitled son, Duke of Kent.

The wedding was one of the finest pieces of pageantry which has ever been staged in this country. All the streets on the route to and from Westminster Abbey were festooned with flags and bunting, and the West End was similarly decorated.

The fact that Christmas was only a month away helped, but it wasn't really necessary to swell the fervour or the excited adulation of the crowds, who had taken this foreign princess to be their own. The pomp and pageantry far excelled the wedding of our present Queen to the Duke of Edinburgh, for their marriage came so soon after the end of the Second World War, during a period of continuing austerity, that no one seemed able to make up their minds as to the way the event should be staged. Even the two coronations which followed paled by comparison. The procession was the fastest ever recorded, though few were aware of this. A threat on the life of Prince Paul, now regent of Yugoslavia and the bride's brother-in-law, had been received by Scotland Yard, so rather than spoil the proceedings with an assassination, every possible precaution was taken, and taken successfully, for the wedding went without a hitch.

After their honeymoon, the bride and groom set up home at 3 Belgrave Square. It was a furnished house, but the Duke took over, had it redecorated, had much of the old furniture moved out and their own put in. A year later, Coppins, their country home, was left to them, and this too he set about with enthusiasm. It was the Duke and not the Duchess who ran the homes and she was content to let him do so. Indeed, she turned out to be a docile wife to a man who was not all that easy to live with. He could be bad-tempered, lacked patience, and, as I've said, was moody and suffered from sleeplessness. She, however, took no notice of his failings. She loved him for what he was, and since by nature she was a little lazy, it suited her to give in to his whims. On the other hand, this didn't train her very well for the confidence she needed when carrying out her public duties. When she was called upon to make her first public speech, a short one at that, she suffered agonies of stage fright. It was to be the same all her life. She was an easy, home-loving person, who adored children, of whom she was to have three, got on well with the other British royals, and naturally remained close to her Greek and

other foreign friends and relations. In the presence of strangers or casual acquaintances, however, she was ill at ease –
call it shyness if you will – which was interpreted by many as
haughtiness; she was considered by some to see herself as
more royal than the Queen and the other ladies of the court.
In my opinion and experience it was a mixture of the two. At
times she would treat her servants almost as members of the
family, but at others it was almost as if we didn't exist.

The great influence the Princess had on public taste, to
Miss Arter's joy, was on fashion. Before her entry on the
scene it was the royal men who had taken the lead in this
respect, the Prince Regent, King Edward VII, and the Duke of
Windsor as Prince of Wales. Victoria never influenced
fashion, and who could imagine anyone following the lead of
Queen Mary the Queen Mother, whose dress sense was
always a matter of controversy? Indeed, our present Queen,
even when younger, failed to attract the attention of the
fashion conscious. Marina, from the moment she appeared in
her pillbox hat, set trends that were copied the world over.
Even before entering her service, when she was only a name
to me, I was aware of her reputation for dresses and hats and
the colour she was known for: Marina blue.

Madame Vernier was the hat queen. Some years later I
visited her with my wife Shirley to collect something and, as a
result of what was by then a long association, she asked
Shirley if she would like one of her creations. We were taken
to her salon and presented with a pale blue and grey one.
Madame reminded me of the actress Yvonne Arnaud, with
that same charming French accent.

It was Miss Arter who opened my eyes to what is normally
a feminine preserve. She explained that although the Princess
wore mainly plain, simple clothes, this plainness was decep-
tive. Her outfits were the result of hours of work and countless fittings. Her day dresses were of simple cut, but her ball
dresses were exotic, full-skirted creations. Her fashion sense
reflected great credit on the dressmakers she used, and of

course she was charged much less than those customers who followed her example.

Oddly enough, I came eventually to be on easy terms with Miss Arter. Apparently few did, for she kept herself very much to herself. Some time after I had left service she had an unfortunate accident. She put her hand on an electric fire and burned it severely. The Princess made sure she had the best medical attention. But that sort of kindness had not always been the case. They often had a set-to. There was one occasion when Her Royal Highness was taking a bath and Edith called to ask her what dress she would be wearing. I was close at hand and could overhear the exchange.

'She says she'll wear the black,' I told her.

'You know, Peter,' Edith said, 'she has six black frocks. Which one does she mean? Am I supposed to be able to read her mind?'

'I should put them all out if I were you,' was my advice. Apparently this did not please.

Later, towards the end of the year, the Princess said, 'Oh Edith, we were discussing Christmas presents. What would you like?'

'Well, your Royal Highness, I think I should be seeing better. I'd like a new pair of glasses.'

This was greeted with 'Mm, mm, don't you think a hearing aid might be more appropriate, in view of the difficulty we have had in communication?'

Edith knew that if she was to preserve the relationship of servant and mistress, she had better bite her tongue. She was, however, in a black mood for two or three days, thinking, I'm sure, of all the things she would have liked to have said.

Poor Edith. In 1958 she retired to a small room or bed-sit, rent paid by Marina, in Brixton. A lonely soul, she lived there until she was eighty. The last time I saw her she didn't know me. She was replaced by another Edith, Edith Henman.

Some lady's maids were toffee-nosed. No one more so than Bobo, the Queen's maid. There was a time when, if the staff ran into her in the corridor, they didn't speak unless she spoke to them. She acted as if she were as royal as the Queen herself. It shows how the chain of command flourished among servants.

A thing that astonished me, in view of the importance the Princess attached to time-keeping during the years I was with her, was that in her married days it was her unpunctuality which probably chiefly irritated the Duke. Queen Mary had always insisted that no matter at what hour her sons had arrived home, or in what condition, they had to present themselves promptly at 8.30 at the breakfast table. Old habits die hard. Bysouth seemed to think that this emphasis on punctuality was one of the ways the Princess kept the Duke's memory alive.

The event in the prewar years which threw the Court and the country back on its heels was, of course, the abdication of Edward, Prince of Wales. It was a topic of conversation that continued throughout my service and I dare say it still sets servants' tongues wagging. Both the Duke and Marina had seen a lot of Edward and Mrs Simpson at Fort Belvedere. She had had tea with them at Coppins and had dined at Belgrave Square, so, as Bysouth said, the Duke and Duchess must have known early of the Prince's intentions. The Duke cancelled all his engagements during the crisis that preceded the abdication, so he could be near his elder brother should he be needed. Both he and Marina were heartbroken at the thought that by agreeing to leave the country the Prince would no longer be part of their lives. So much has been written and said about the Windsors that I feel I can add little, even from servants' hall gossip. I do know that Mrs Simpson was unpopular with the staff of the houses she visited. Her wit and sophistication may have attracted the Prince of Wales, but she had a habit of being bitchily smart at servants' expense. Some in secure positions and held in esteem by their employers were able to retaliate as only good butlers know how. Others had to take it on the chin.

One of our housemaids, Jessie McCreedy, had been in service at Fort Belvedere at the time of the abdication. In a tragic voice she described how it was she who opened and shut the door of the Fort when the Prince left; apparently the. butler was too overcome at the time. Her eyes welled with tears as she described the experience. It didn't impress Bysouth. 'If I had as many pounds as times I've heard that story from servants, I should have retired years ago.'

Near the end of 1938 came a piece of news which, while it delighted the Duke, caused the Duchess some misgivings. King George VI announced that he was sending them both to Australia where the Duke would be governor general, succeeding Lord Gowrie. The reason the Princess was not enthusiastic was that it meant putting a great distance between her and her mother and sisters, whom she loved so dearly, and with whom she had been able to exchange visits regularly.

Australians were delighted with the appointment, not least because they loved the look of the glamorous Duchess whom the Duke would be bringing with him. If she wasn't too keen on the idea, her feelings were as nothing compared with those of the dress designers and manufacturers for whom it spelt disaster. For the first time they had wrested the couture lead from the Parisians and now they could see an end to this domination.

There was much to keep the Princess busy once the initial disappointment was over. In August 1939 they were in Yugoslavia, saying their farewells to her mother and sister, when the Duke, disturbed by the undertones of war, decided to return home. A day or two later he cabled Marina to come at once. When war was declared in September 1939, it was decided that his Australian appointment would have to be delayed.

At first he went to the Admiralty, but he disliked being confined to a desk and transferred to the RAF. He gave up the house in Belgrave Square and they all moved to Coppins. The

Duchess was called upon to play her part; she was appointed Commandant of the WRNS. There are many who believe that it was her appearance in uniform which was the greatest filip for recruitment that the service had. Inevitably she decided that the floppy hats, a legacy of the First World War, were unattractive, so new designs were made and the final selection was gratefully received by the girls.

A story she was very fond of telling in the years after the war was how, when she was inspecting a WRNS unit, she noticed that there was a contingent of foreign sailors stationed nearby.

'Don't they disturb you?' she inquired.

'Oh, no, only at night,' was the reply.

Although the Duke's duties with the RAF took him around the country inspecting factories and generally doing a public-relations job, he again became restless. He wanted to experience more of the action and said so repeatedly. His wishes were in part granted, and he flew to Canada to report on an air-training scheme. He fancied getting some sort of job with the United States Air Force. He was next sent to Ireland to visit our units there, but he was also going to combine it with a visit to an American base. On 25 August 1942 he took off from Scotland in a flying boat, which crashed into a mountain some thirty minutes later, killing all on board, except the rear gunner. It was the faithful Foxy who broke the news to Marina.

With that tragic aircrash ended what had promised to be one of the happiest of royal marriages. It clearly affected Princess Marina deeply for it seemed to change not only her life style but her character. It was this character that I was to work for for the next three years. I got to know more about her, her habits, her likes and dislikes. But I never really got to know her. There was something secret and inscrutable about her that was only shown to the close and favoured few.

FOUR

Most people believe that any member of the royal family is automatically well breeched. Before her marriage, Princess Marina probably had little worry over money. Indeed, until the Duke's death, I don't suppose she gave it much thought, even though he regularly rebuked her about the size of the phone bill and asked her to limit the time she spent talking to her mother and sisters, who were living abroad. As with most women, that kind of criticism went in one ear and out of the other.

After his death, when she was in the driving seat as it were, it was brought home to her how relatively poor she really was. Being so young, it had never occurred to the Duke to make any provision for his wife, although he left some money in trust for his children. His annuity from the Civil List had been £25,000 a year, a very fair income at that time, but it died with him. He had been left a fifth of George V's money, but he had spent most of this on various antiques, silver, pictures and *objets d'art*. So Marina found herself short of ready money. At first the King helped out, as did Queen Mary, but to the Princess this smacked of charity and she hated having to accept it.

Parliament, in a period of austerity, was in no mood to grant her anything, so she decided that the only thing to do was to sell some of the art treasures which her husband had collected. The sale fetched around £90,000 and was positive proof that the Duke had known what he was doing when he made his purchases. My description of Kensington Palace shows that there were many beautiful things remaining, but almost all of these had to go in a further sale in 1960. In 1952 the Civil List was revised and Marina received £5000 a year, though this in no way completely relieved the problems.

One result of her comparative poverty was that by making drastic economies she was considered mean by some. It was known, for instance, that she had agreements with couturiers that they would lend a dress specially designed for her, on the understanding that she would return it immediately and they could sell it to another customer who was pleased to pay over the odds for something that Marina had recently worn. It was not the kind of thing that was normally done by the upper classes even, let alone royalty.

She also saved money by paring the housekeeping to the bone, causing groans in the kitchen by reprimanding us if she considered too much food had been prepared for lunch. How were we to guess the size of the royal appetite that day? I remember her saying that we must wait until strawberries were in season before serving them. 'They're so expensive otherwise and we really can't afford it.' She might have saved a bob or two by such economies, but scarcely a day would pass without her squandering money on something we could have well done without, like the butter sent from Windsor with its 'fare' in the baggage van paid for. She also kept the servants' money to a minimum, relying on our willingness to work for salaries considered low even in those days. If you suggested a rise, it was as though you were asking for the moon. I got two increases of 5s. a week while I was with her, and I wouldn't have got those if I hadn't asked for them.

Money apart, there were other considerations that affected her character after her husband's death. Like many beautiful and spoiled women, she had played on these characteristics over the years. She had pretended not to understand worldly things. Now that she had to stand firmly on her own two feet, she was forced to make up for lost time. It was, I believe, her memory of the Duke which gave her the resolve, that and her 'good breeding'. She determined that the kind of work he had engaged in would not be forgotten; she took over as many of her husband's public duties as she was able. In the end she was concerned with over a hundred organizations and in many she took a personal and active interest. One, of course, which springs easily to mind, was her presidency of the All-England Lawn Tennis Club at Wimbledon.

Naturally, as in any job, there were routine chores. Listening in to the conversations the Duchess had with her lady's maid before performing such duties gave me many a chuckle. Here she is talking to her lady-in-waiting, Constance.

'Where am I going this afternoon, Constance?'

'Ma'am, you're going to, ahem, I think it's SE6.'

'That means nothing to me, I'm afraid, Constance. Where is SE6?'

'I'm afraid I don't know either.'

'Well, hadn't you better find out?'

'Well, ma'am, I thought we could rely on Freddy. He's bound to know.'

'I should make sure he does, eh, don't you think?'

'Very well, ma'am. I'll make a note of it.'

'Good. Well, now, what do I do when I get to SE – what number did you say?'

'Six, ma'am.'

'Ah, yes, six. What do I do there?'

'It's an orphanage, and also combines an old people's complex. You're opening a new wing and attending a bazaar.'

'I see. Tell me, do I have to make a speech on this occasion?'

'Well, yes, ma'am, you have to say a few words.'

'Oh, dear. You know how I hate it.'

'Yes, I do know, ma'am, but Philip [Hay] has had something typed out for you.'

'Where is it?'

'Here, ma'am.'

Marina glances through it. 'Mm. Philip is so good at this sort of thing. Keep it safely, whatever you do. I'll have another look at it in the car.'

'Yes, ma'am. You've no doubt noticed that when you arrive you've got to say you remember coming there on a previous occasion.'

'But that's the trouble, you see, Constance, I don't.'

'Perhaps you will when you get there. Anyway, you'll have to pretend you do because you have. I've made some notes to remind you. You went in 1949 when it first opened and you very graciously introduced a new matron whom you'd previously met at another old people's home.'

'Oh, Lord, Constance, how am I expected to remember? First SE6, then a home for old people, an orphanage, and now a matron. I recall none of it.'

'I know, it isn't easy for you, ma'am.'

'Not easy is an understatement, Constance. It's impossible.'

'Yes, ma'am. But if I may go on, the matron's name is Miss Elverston and she's getting on in years. I understand she's grown a bit fat and may find it difficult to curtsey. You see, she also suffers from, er, an arthritic condition.'

'It sounds to me as if she should be one of the inmates, not running the show, if you know what I mean, eh? Anyway, if she can't curtsey, I shall ignore it.'

'That's very gracious of you, ma'am.'

'You said something about a bazaar. Shall I be expected to buy anything?'

'Well, it would be a nice gesture, and much appreciated, I'm sure, ma'am. Perhaps, as it's getting near Christmas, you may see something for one of the servants.'

'Mmm, mmm, mmm. Then make sure you have some money handy, Constance. I shan't want to spend much though. Oh, by the way, do I have to shake many hands?'

'Well, you know how the old people like it.'

'Very well, then make sure you take two pairs of gloves, won't you?'

'I've already prepared for that, ma'am.'

'Good. That seems to be all, except for this SE6. You will make sure Freddy knows?'

'Yes, ma'am.'

The Princess had two ladies-in-waiting while I was with her, Lady Constance Milnes-Gaskell and Lady Mary Rachel Davidson, sister of the Duke of Norfolk. Lady Mary's husband was killed during the war, and she later remarried Brigadier Anthony Pepys, a descendant of Samuel Pepys. Both ladies were very close friends of the Duchess and were almost part of the family. I say almost because, if she was entertaining personal friends, they would make themselves scarce. On other formal occasions they would assist her as hostesses. Normally they did one month on, one month off, for theirs could be a very busy life, particularly if they had their own entertaining to do. For the staff, they could be an added burden, since if they required anything, they didn't hesitate to demand it. From what I heard, though, from visiting servants, we were fortunate in having two reasonably considerate ladies to look after.

Marina also seemed to rely a good deal on her private secretary, Philip Hay, for his advice and judgement. For instance, he would address staff members about things that Her Royal Highness wanted done, but one felt that he had probably made the suggestions to her in the first place. His wife had been lady-in-waiting to the Queen and, I imagine, provided a valuable source of back-door information.

Most of the formal entertaining was done at Kensington Palace; only family or personal friends were invited to Coppins. It astonished me that the Princess never entertained anyone from the town of Iver. To the Cockney boy in me, neighbours had always been an important part of life. Indeed, the Princess never went into town except to church on the occasional Sunday. She was on courteous terms with the local vicar, but the moment she walked out of the churchyard that was it.

I quickly got the hang of serving food in the correct fashion, and I can honestly say that, unlike one footman I knew, I never caused a potato to be dropped into a lady's cleavage.

The footman concerned was lucky, for it is normally a court-martial offence. His victim was a young lady, very free with her opinions at the dinner table, to the annoyance of her hostess and friends. She was also given to using gestures to make her point, and it was during one of these that she knocked the spoon that the footman had positioned for her on a potato dish. It was like potting a billiard ball. The potato went straight onto her naked skin just above the edge of her low-cut dress. The trouble was the lady lost her nerve and, instead of flicking it out, she put up her hand and squashed it into her bosom. 'And as you know, Peter,' the footman told me, 'while potatoes may be hot outside, they are scalding inside. She screamed with pain, called me an unrepeatable name and dashed out of the room. Well, I stood rooted to the ground, feeling no end of a Charlie, expecting the biggest rocket ever, if not instant dismissal. Instead the whole table, including my Lady, began roaring with laughter, and someone shouted, "Well done, my man. That's the first time I've seen anyone hole in one." The butler, however, did not seem amused and he whispered to me to make myself scarce for the rest of the meal. He later tried giving me a wigging, but even he was unable to keep a straight face, so I got off light.'

The occasion which I've always considered my greatest test – and my finest hour – was a tea party at Kensington Palace. I'd only been with the Duchess for a short time when Bysouth developed raging toothache just after lunch. He spoke about it to Her Royal Highness and she sent him off post haste to the dentist.

'But what about tea?' he asked.

'Don't worry about that. Peter will have to serve it.'

At first, when he told me, it caused me little concern, but then he recited the list of visitors, and my heart missed a beat or two.

'There will be the Queen Mother, the Princess Royal, Lord Mountbatten, and the Lords Tedder and Montgomery.'

'Gawd,' I said. 'What's it going to be, a bloody council of war?'

Bysouth's face didn't change, which was probably just as well because it had by now blown up like a balloon on one side. 'Just do what I've told you and everything will be all right. Remember to give them the full treatment.' And he then was off.

I had the kettle on the boil all afternoon, and I must have laid and relaid the tea trolley some two or three times. Then I started rehearsing handing round the plates with little lace serviettes and cake knives. There were to be two pots of tea, India and China, poured from silver Georgian teapots, with water kept at near boiling point in a silver kettle on a methylated spirit burner. There were milk and cream jugs, teastrainers, lemon slices, a collation of sugar cubes and crystals, crumpets resting on a hot-water container, brown and white bread and butter, strawberry and apricot jam, fresh honey straight from the bees, and the inevitable cucumber sandwiches. There were chocolate cakes and chocolate fingers, a bowl of fruit, and fingerbowls, and finally the silver-cased notepad and pencil which I hoped the Princess would have no cause to use that afternoon.

At around half past three Mum rang up with the exciting news that Aunt Agnes was going to tea with my two cousins. When I went through our guest list she didn't seem particularly impressed.

'Not very many of 'em, Peter. I'm sure you'll be able to manage.'

'No, Mum, I agree, not very many, but what they lack in quantity, they make up in quality.'

When at last I felt I'd done all that I could, I waited near the phone for a call from Clarence House to tell me that the Queen Mother was leaving. This was common practice and I could now tell almost to the second at what time she would arrive. It was important, for the front door was always open for her so that she could walk straight in. It was the same for the Queen and Prince Philip. All other guests, royal or not, found the door shut, and would have to ring for someone to admit them.

Though I say it myself, the tea party went well, and not once did I see Marina make a note on her pad. Although she had an official appointment at 6.30, I was not worried since I knew that, with the Queen Mother there, her car would arrive at the front door at 5.30 precisely, and that it would be followed by the Princess Royal's car. It was a matter of no consequence to me in what way the army, navy and air force left. They could sort themselves out in order of seniority if they so wished.

There is a routine which butlers have to observe if guests look like overstaying their welcome. With the hierarchy, it is understood that when the butler opens the sitting-room door, it is time for them to get up and move. Other more obstinate visitors are got rid of by announcing that their cars are outside waiting, and instantly the hostess rises and makes her adieux.

By the time our guests had left, Bysouth had returned, looking just as horrible, but obviously no longer in pain. When the drawing-room bell went, however, he said he was in no shape to answer it, and I could see his point. When I went into the room the Duchess looked up at me and said, 'I want to congratulate you on the way you served tea this afternoon, Peter. I realize it must have been an ordeal for you and you acquitted yourself very well indeed.'

'What did she want?' Bysouth asked when I returned.

'Oh, nothing of any importance, she just thought a table was out of place and wanted it moved, that's all.'

'Typical,' said Bysouth. 'Never really satisfied, women.'

I could hardly wait to tell Mum that I thought I had proved myself at least in the eyes of my employer.

The Princess was a lover of good music and the theatre, not so much the classical stuff but good West End dramas and comedies. She was friendly with Douglas Fairbanks, Noël Coward and Sir Malcolm Sargent in particular, and they dined frequently at Kensington Palace and Coppins. I particularly enjoyed Noël Coward's visits, for as well as his sparkling and witty conversation, he would play the piano and sing. Normally the piano was kept in Princess Alexandra's sitting room in Kensington Palace or the drawing room at Coppins, so we always knew when he was expected because we had to make sure it was well polished. For some reason or other Bysouth hated him, couldn't stand his voice or his music, and said so loudly in the servants' quarters.

'If you don't like it, why don't you stuff your ears with cotton wool?' Eileen Hennessy, Marina's head housemaid, said.

'Or get yourself a pair of earmuffs,' added another housemaid.

Bysouth said that the reason he couldn't come to terms with Coward was that he wrote about servants as though they were a bunch of ignoramuses, a common lot who would forget their training at the drop of an aitch.

'He ought to know better, he hangs around here so often, you would have thought he could've got it right by now. I shall tell him so one of these days, you mark my words.'

And he did one evening, when he was helping him into his coat. To his astonishment, Mr Coward took it on the chin.

'There's a lot in what you say, Bysouth. Thank you. I will remember it in future.'

From then on Bysouth's attitude towards Noël changed, but he still sniffed whenever he heard his music.

For my part, I couldn't hear enough. I found myself hanging on his words at the dinner table, which is a fatal thing for any servant to do. No matter how hard you may try to disguise it, it is obvious to everyone that you are listening in on the conversation. According to Bysouth, it is the eyes that give you away. However, I threw discretion to the wind and when, after dinner, Mr Noël started to perform, I would make my way to the drawing room and potter around on the slightest pretext. I particularly remember one night when Marina asked him if he knew any of Ivor Novello's melodies; he made a *moue*, but proceeded to oblige. He was playing something from *The Dancing Years*, when Prince Edward's dog Columbus went up to the piano, cocked his leg and piddled. Noël stopped, threw his hands up in the air in delight and said, 'You see, not only an actor but a critic.'

The story I heard about him which I believe to be one of the best-off-the-cuff remarks I've ever come across was on the day of our Queen's coronation. Mr Noël was one of a party sitting on a balcony overlooking the route. There had been the usual outburst of excitement as the Queen and Prince Philip rode by, and after that it seemed as if everything would be an anticlimax. Then a carriage appeared carrying a massive jet-black figure.

'Who on earth is that?' exclaimed one of the party.

'Oh, that's Queen Salote of Tonga,' answered another.

Seated beside her was the small figure of her prime minister.

'And who's that with her?'

'Oh that's her lunch,' Noël replied quickly, and the balcony nearly gave way as the party collapsed with laughter.

Bysouth's antipathy to Noël Coward went deeper than the man or his music. He was of the old school, brought up on Victorian ballads and Gilbert and Sullivan. He was given to bursting into song on the slightest pretext and, to be fair, he had a full, resonant baritone voice, so resonant in fact that it could be heard in the dining room. One morning we were expecting Queen Juliana and Princess Beatrix of the Netherlands, Lord and Lady Louis Mountbatten and a few others.

While he was laying the table, Bysouth burst into the
'Toreador Song' from *Carmen*, which is a piercing piece
at the best of times, and he was giving it the fullest treatment.
I answered the bell from the drawing room. The Princess,
who was smiling, asked if I would kindly request Bysouth to
go and see her. I had more than an inkling of what it was
about, and was interested to know how she would broach the
subject. Against all the rules, I eavesdropped outside the
door.

'Ah, Bysouth,' I heard her say. 'I thought I could hear some
singing coming from somewhere, which, though pleasant,
seemed more than a trifle loud. I wonder if you would tell
whoever it was to modulate their voice a little. We don't want
our guests disturbed, do we?'

'I will attend to the matter, your Royal Highness,' Bysouth
replied. 'And I apologize on behalf of whoever it was that you
have been disturbed.'

'Thank you, Bysouth. That will be all.'

You cringing two-faced bugger, I thought to myself as I
quickly vamoosed behind the door.

'No taste for real music, the Duchess,' Bysouth remarked a
couple of days later. 'Only interested in this new-fangled
stuff.'

As it happens, this was untrue and he knew it, for another
regular visitor was Sir Malcolm Sargent. A bit of a dandy I
thought him, always appearing with a red carnation in his
buttonhole and spending a good minute examining himself in
front of the mirror, straightening his jacket and fiddling with
his tie before allowing Bysouth or myself to announce him.
Still, he was an affable enough chap and seemed a good
conversationalist, though I didn't usually trouble to listen to
what he was saying. I probably wouldn't have understood
half of it anyway as he was a bit too square for me.

He was very gallant so far as the ladies were concerned. If
he had been to lunch, hardly half an hour after his departure a
sheaf of flowers would arrive from him. Marina was not as

touched by this gesture as she should have been. I remember a bouquet of two dozen red roses that he sent. I took them into her and was about to remove them and put them in a vase, when she stopped me.

'No, just hold them there,' she said and she went to her boudoir where she wrote a message on a card. She then replaced Sir Malcolm's note with hers and told me to have them sent to Princess Marie Louise in Fitzmaurice Place.

'She's not very well, Peter, and she will appreciate them more than I do.'

Her gesture struck me as being all very fine, but it wasn't what Sir Malcolm had intended.

Somehow the Princess got to hear of my love of the theatre. She was capable of surprising thoughtfulness and she would occasionally recommend shows for me to go and see. Recommendations are all right, but it was finding the time, for I was still a bit of a mother's boy and on my days off I wanted to spend them at home. I looked on it both as a duty and a pleasure. One evening the drawing-room bell went and Marina said that in a few minutes the Bolshoi ballet was appearing on television. Knowing my liking for the theatre, she thought I might like to watch it with her. It was, of course, most kind and considerate, but a more uncomfortable evening I find hard to remember. I knew nothing at all about ballet and after about ten minutes I realized that I didn't want to. I felt most awkward in her presence. I knew how to behave when I was serving her, but I wasn't at all sure of my position when socializing. I sat bolt upright in the chair she had signalled me to sit on. I was too far forward and something seemed to be sticking into my bum, but I didn't like to move. I could sense her eyes straying towards me from time to time to see how I was reacting. I wasn't. Yet, when one of the dancers twirled round or someone threw her in the air and caught her, I heard the Princess gasp with pleasure and clap her hands together. By the end of it I was as exhausted as the dancers with the tension of it all. Thankfully

I rose to my feet, expressed my pleasure and gratitude and made for the staff sitting room, fell into a chair and tried to recover from the strain of it all. It put me off ballet for life and if ever I arrive home to find the family watching it on the box, I'm very firm with them. 'You can switch that bloody stuff off for a start,' is my usual greeting.

Something I learned early in service was 'Never judge a sausage by its skin' – though it wasn't a sausage that I learned it from, but a slice of bacon. One morning just after the Princess's breakfast tray had been taken up, Miss Arter came running into the staff quarters.

'The Princess very much fancies a bit of bacon with her breakfast. Will you please see to it?'

'She'll be lucky,' Bernard, the odd-man, said. 'I've just eaten the last rasher.'

Bysouth was quickly on the ball. 'Peter, go next door to Princess Alice's place and beg some from them.'

I obeyed at the double, went straight into the servants' hall, for I knew their butler, Mr Bentley, well. He wasn't there, but an elderly woman, whom I took to be a maid, was. She was arranging some flowers. I explained briefly our predicament, treating her for what I thought she was. She went to the fridge and handed me a few slices on a plate.

'Ta everso, ma,' I said.

'Give my regards to that old bugger Bentley, and tell him we'll pay him back as soon as possible,' and then I exited fast. It wasn't until a few days later, when we were giving a small tea party, that I realized what a clanger I'd dropped. I opened the door to admit the Earl and Countess of Athlone and there on the Earl's arm was my 'maid'. Her eyes twinkled when she saw me and I did get the chance to whisper my apologies.

'It's quite all right, don't worry. It will remain our secret.'

Later I got to know them quite well and Bentley was able to fill me in on their history.

The Earl had been governor general of South Africa and, during the Second World War, governor general of Canada.

He was the brother of Queen Mary and so was of the House of Teck. Princess Alice was the granddaughter of Queen Victoria, of whom she spoke most highly, denying the stories that she was a stiff and austere old lady. She found her most outgoing and remembered the fun and the laughter whenever she visited the old Queen. Victoria loved playing with her grandchildren, though like all elders at that time she demanded certain standards of behaviour in return.

The Princess was considered unconventional for her time. She had killed a man-eating tiger, donned a diving suit to get a close look at a coral reef, flown in a Zeppelin, travelled in Saudi Arabia wearing native dress; it is also believed that she rode in one of the first tanks to be built. Bentley suspected that, had she not been of royal blood, she would have been one of the earliest supporters of the Suffragettes, and it is certain that Queen Victoria would not have been amused at the support she gave to birth control. She was a strange mixture, for she took her royal duties most seriously and it is doubtful if anyone will equal her record of 20,000 official engagements. It is also doubtful if anyone will live so long. For she was ninety-seven when she died in January 1981. She remained a confidante and a critic of the family until the last. She was supposed to have reprimanded the Queen Mother for smiling too much, Charles and Anne for their sloppy deportment. She also disliked headscarves, which so many ladies, including the Queen, frequently wore. I know Princess Marina used to slink out of the palace if she was going for a stroll in order not to give offence. Altogether, my 'char' was a great and distinguished lady with an influence that few people ever realized.

There was another bond between Princess Alice and me. She always bought her flowers from a street flower-seller called Ada Shakespeare, in Kensington, and so did I if I was called upon to get some for table decorations. Apparently the Princess grew very fond of Ada, and they would chat together whenever they met. I heard of this and mentioned it to Mum.

'There was a Shakespeare on your father's side. She may well be connected with them,' she said excitedly. Well, Shakespeare is an uncommon name, except around Stratford-on-Avon, so next time I saw Ada we chatted about it. Mum was right. It turned out that she was some sort of second cousin once removed, so she said, but I could never quite understand the removed bit. Since that time, we always remained on friendly terms, even after I left service. When a short time ago I heard that she had died, I thought Princess Alice should know, so I wrote to her. I had a reply by return. She had heard the news, and was very saddened at the loss of a dear friend. It was only ten months before she herself died.

Security played its part in our lives. There were always police outside the palace both night and day and they questioned anyone who approached either the front or back doors. On occasions the Princess was impatient at the care that was taken of her. She would put on her oldest clothes, tie on a headscarf, and walk in Kensington Gardens incognito. While the police accepted this desire for privacy, there was one time when they were worried about her excursions. 'There have been one or two flashers around the park recently, and we've had several complaints. Let's hope she doesn't run into one of 'em.' I mentioned it to Bysouth, who again demonstrated his surprising sense of humour.

'Yes, I've heard about it,' he remarked. 'There was a case the other day when three old ladies were on a seat in the park, and some geyser opened his dirty mack and exposed himself to them. Nasty business. Two of the old dears had a stroke, the other couldn't reach.' An unpredictable old bugger, Bysouth was.

Shortly after I'd joined, I offended against security precautions. The back-door bell rang and there stood a little old lady clasping a bunch of daffodils wrapped in a piece of newspaper. She had evidently eluded the police. She handed me the flowers and asked if I would be kind enough to give them to Princess Marina, for whom she had such a deep admiration. 'A beautiful courageous woman,' she said. 'She, like me, lost her husband in action, though mine was killed in the First World War.' She seemed such a dear old soul, I did what Mum would have done under the circumstances, I asked her if she would like a cup of tea. It was as though I had offered her the Crown Jewels and her eyes sparkled with pride and delight. We were enjoying a chat, when in walked the Princess.

'Ah, Peter . . .' she began, then saw the old lady, and stretched out to shake her hand, assuming she was my mother. I hastily explained the situation. She took the daffodils and put them in a vase, thanking the old lady whose cup was now full as she dropped a curtsey and made her exit.

It wasn't until later that evening that the matter came up. Bysouth called me to his pantry and said, 'Well, while the Duchess was delighted to meet that lady this afternoon, I've been instructed by Mr Hay to tell you that it's something that must never be repeated. It's a rule of the palace that no strangers are ever admitted on any pretext whatsoever. You should, in this instance, have called the police. You will not, however, mention anything of what I've said to the Princess, who, it seems, was most touched by the old lady's behaviour.'

It was strange that at Coppins there was no round-the-clock guard by the police. The only time they were present was when the Queen and Prince Philip, or the Queen Mother, were expected. I was surprised there one day when a man came up to me in the garden and asked to see her Royal Highness. He was well dressed and wore a white carnation in his buttonhole. I asked him if he had an appointment.

'No,' he replied. 'But I'm sure she'll be only too glad that I'm here. You see, I'm in love with her.'

Now, that set me right back on my heels. What, I wondered, does one say now? In the event I thought I did rather well.

'She has many admirers, sir. I will just see if the Princess will receive you. If you will, please remain here . . .'

Once indoors, I made it fast to the telephone and the police were with us in a matter of minutes, during which time I returned to the garden and listened to the babblings of a madman. 'I really just called to settle the arrangements for the wedding.' It was stuff like that. Pathetic, of course, and I felt wretched as he was bundled into the police car, but what else could I have done?

The townsfolk of Iver were often of help, particularly as far as the press were concerned. Newspaper men seem to make their presence known at the local pubs and, even if they don't say where they're from, they're like plain-clothes coppers, almost instantly recognizable by the well-informed. So we generally had early warning if any were seen around the town.

I haven't mentioned much about Coppins. I don't intend taking you on a tour of the house, it gets rather exhausting. The Duke, Marina's husband, referred to it as their country cottage, but that, if I may say so, was inverted snobbery, though it is more common these days so to describe some twenty-roomed mansion. Though Coppins was far from being a cottage, inside it had all the appearances of a home. It was an ugly Victorian building, left to the Duke by Princess Victoria, daughter of Edward VII. When the Kents took over they found that most of the furniture and the fittings were as nasty as the exterior and the garden overgrown with trees, laurels and holly. They set about combining elegance with a homelike quality. There were two sitting rooms, both spacious and gay, a dining room, a music room and about six bedrooms, with a nursery and ample staff quarters. I was disappointed in the room I was given. It was smaller and in no way as attractive as the one at Kensington Palace. Still, it was tolerable, and since we were at Coppins for the late spring and summer, there were compensations.

In the entrance hall was a marble bust of Edward VII, one of the few bits of Princess Victoria's legacy that was allowed to remain. It was an austere piece, not at all representative of the randy dog history has made him out to be. Alice, the housemaid, would chat to it when she was cleaning the hall of a morning. I caught her at it several times, and began to hide so that I could listen.

' 'Allo, you old bugger. 'Ow are you today? Look a bit down in the mouth. What's the matter, dearie, old age creepin' up on yer? Findin' yer 'ard up fer a bit of the other? Comes to all of us, luvvie. Not that I give it credence, not from all the accounts I 'ear. They all say you're a dirty old sod, and always chasing a bit of fluff' – and so she would go on.

Sometimes she would pretend to be sorry for him. 'If ever you get a bit hard up for it, you know where to come, don't you, duck?'

One day Bysouth caught her at it, and told her it was lese-majesty (I wasn't sure what that meant) and she would end up in the Tower of London. It didn't have the effect he had hoped. She brightened up no end.

'What, wiv all them luvly Beefeaters? I should be so lucky.'

Like Kensington Palace, the rooms at Coppins were chintzy and beautifully furnished, but with lighter and more fragile pieces, Chippendale or pale pine. Much of the silver and a few precious ornaments were brought down specially from Kensington Palace.

The only parts of the house that were not modernized were the kitchen and the servants' quarters. The kitchen had a heavy stone floor which was hard on the feet. Apparently it got very hot in summer, or so one chef found. There came a morning when the sitting-room bell went, and Marina asked me to send the chef to her as there were some alterations she wished to make to the menu. He had only returned to the kitchen some thirty seconds when the bell rang again.

'Ah, Peter, tell me, did you look at the chef's feet before you showed him in?'

'No, your Royal Highness, it is not my habit to study people's feet at any time. The chef's general demeanour

seemed to me to be satisfactory. Was there something wrong
with his feet?'

'There most certainly was, Peter. He came into my drawing
room barefooted and, from the condition of them, they
appeared most unsavoury.'

I must admit that I was a bit shaken at the chef's stupidity.
However, I thought I would help to fight from his corner.
'It's the kitchen floor, your Royal Highness. It gets very hot in
the summer, and you know chefs are something of a law unto
themselves.'

'I don't like it. I don't like it one little bit. Please tell him
that at all times he must have his feet covered.'

I'm afraid I couldn't resist it. 'I will carry out your instructions, your Royal Highess, but I feel I must point out that
your food is prepared with his hands, not his feet.'

It didn't get either of us anywhere. The Princess was dis-
tinctly frosty towards me for the next few days, and by the
end of the following week we were looking for a new chef.

In fact, cooks and chefs came and went with great regular-
ity. I think many of them came, as indeed did the housemaids,
expecting, like Dick Whittington, to find the house paved
with gold and the saucepan handles decorated with
diamonds, only to be disillusioned the moment they entered
the staff quarters. This kind of servant didn't stay long, just
long enough to say they had been in royal service. The basic
staff at Coppins consisted of Bysouth, myself, the chef or
cook, the lady's maids, a head housekeeper, daily housemaids and cleaners who came from Iver, and of course the
two chauffeurs.

The gardens at Coppins were most attractive. We employed two gardeners. There was, of course, a tennis court,
and in a corner of the garden a sandpit with various swings,
seesaws and the like which the children had used when they
were younger and which still kept visiting children and, later,
grandchildren amused. The rose garden was Marina's pride
and joy. It was at the end of what was called 'the middle

avenue' and was approached through a pair of wrought-iron gates. It was square with rose bushes grouped at various levels on either side of crazy-paving paths. There was a wooden seat which had been a favourite resting place for the Duke and Duchess when he was alive. Often, in the early evening, if we were trying to find her, we would see her sitting there in a kind of brown study and Miss Arter would whisper that she was reliving her days with the Duke.

Weekends at Iver were times we didn't look forward to. The children more or less took over and Marina was only too happy that they should as, when the Duke was alive, and was asked what they did at Coppins at the weekend, he invariably replied, 'We play with the children.' So, it was an unwritten rule that Marina had inherited. It was also something of which the children took full advantage, and there always seemed to be a party of some kind planned, often with as many as twenty guests. This meant not only arranging the guest rooms but also the unoccupied staff bedrooms when visitors were staying the night, and decisions on this might be made at the very last minute. Sometimes extra staff were required, and it was only then that the Princess would voice any criticism, for extra staff meant extra expense, not only on their wages, but on their return fares from London, and on the cars that had to be laid on to shuttle them from and to the station at Iver. But though it meant extra work, and like the rest of the staff, I belly-ached at that, there was much about those weekends that I enjoyed. Coppins used to come alive. There was laughter, music and the babble of young voices, and that seemed to me what country-house life was supposed to be all about.

When I first joined, Princess Alexandra had already had her coming-out party. From what I had heard, I was disappointed to have missed it, until I met a butler who had experienced another such event as a young footman.

'It's something you can well do without,' he told me. 'All right, it's quite fun at the beginning, with the decorated

marquees, the fairy lights, champagne, a couple of bands, the
tiaras, the jewels, the lot, and the food is always provided by
outside caterers, so all you have to do is to hand out drinks
and watch out for gate-crashers. But to see people smothered
in diamonds when they're half pissed, skirts hoisted, eating
bacon and eggs on the stairs at five in the morning, is a quaint
and jaundice-making sight, as I remember. And as if that
wasn't sufficient, when I staggered up to bed, unsteady with
exhaustion, not drink, picking my way through sprawling
couples, thinking how unattractive second-hand love can be,
and opened the door of my room to find two of them in my
bed, I'd had more than enough. There was this couple going
at it like knives. My being there didn't seem to disturb them.
The brazen little girl turned her head on my pillow and
looked at me with what normally I would have taken for
innocent eyes. "Oh," she murmured, cool as you like, "is the
party over?"

' "This one is for you," I said, giving her the haughty
treatment. "Now get yourself out before I ring the fire alarm
and have you put out."

'No, Peter, take my experience to heart, it's not something
you need worry about having missed; though, of course,
come to think of it, many's the drink I've been bought for
telling the story of what the footman saw.'

I took the hint and poured him a good slug of Her Royal
Highness's brandy.

Bysouth watched the drinks supply very carefully. He kept
the key of the wine cupboard and it was difficult to prise it
from him. It wasn't until he realized that I had no particular
taste for the stuff that he allowed me easier access. Of
course, in the old days there was always a cask of beer kept
for the servants, which was doled out to all, regardless of sex.
It was a relic of the days when tea and coffee were expensive
luxuries and beer the drink of the working class. In those
days it was taken with breakfast and at intervals during the
day. Then, with the coming of temperance and with cheaper

tea, though it was the sweepings that servants had, it was decided that those who didn't drink should get beer money instead. How that concession was granted, heaven alone knows, for there never was a trade union for servants. It was too good to last and, on the pretext that beer money was combined with wages, discontinued.

Bysouth kept bottles of beer which he doled out like a man with no arms. Occasionally, if he considered it a festive occasion, he would allow us a drink, and if Mrs Bysouth and he had words in the afternoon he would ask me to join him in a beer or a cup of tea; but he was such a doleful companion at those times that as often as not I would refuse, pretending that I had too much work to do. He would also offer drinks as bribes to the chauffeurs if there was any danger of Marina being back late, which was of course a right royal nuisance. 'You see she's back here by such and such an hour and there'll be a drop of the best on the end of it,' he'd say.

He was continually suspecting members of the staff of filching from the grog tray. The only time they could have done so was first thing in the morning for there was too much to-ing and fro-ing during the day. He would come into the staff room around breakfast time, sniffing away like a bloodhound. I really felt I had his confidence when he explained how he was able to tell if anyone had been fiddling a drink from a decanter. He took me along to the grog tray.

'Now Peter, if you lift that stopper from the whisky decanter, you'll see that it's dry. That's because no one has poured a drink from it since last night. Now, you pour some whisky into a glass, only a little mind, and put the stopper back. Now take it off again and you'll find it's damp. So, you see, if any of the servants had a quick slurp this morning, I'd know. I'd also know what drink they'd imbibed.'

I found it a useful tip when I myself became a butler. Indeed, I managed to track down the odd offender by following his instructions. Bysouth also taught me how to 'bend' or decant a bottle of port and how to filter both ports and clarets through muslin.

Bysouth was responsible for ordering the wines, spirits and liqueurs. He took over this duty on the death of the Duke, though he had to cut his suit according to Marina's cloth. He bought wisely, and our ports and clarets were of excellent vintage. He boasted that he could sell them for three times what he had paid for them. Some wealthy families did just that, bought in bulk and sold when the price was right, and in that way were able to drink for free. Just another example of how the rich stay rich. We also had a running stock of hocks and white Burgundies. Not unnaturally, I thought that the Princess would like Greek wines, such as retsina, which I could never stomach, or drink the occasional glass of ouzo, but she had been introduced to wine from France. That, and the German whites, was what she enjoyed, though she was abstemious.

During the summer months while we were at Coppins a skeleton staff kept Kensington Palace running. Sometimes, however, for a special occasion we would all rush back to town to open up the palace. Probably because Bysouth did not like leaving his cottage at Iver this came to be looked on as my job. I particularly remember one day when Marina had a late afternoon engagement in London. She was having one of her economy drives at the time, and as the cook was at Coppins and there would be no one to prepare a dainty lunch for her at the palace, she decided to take a picnic.

'But, your Royal Highness, where do you intend to stop and eat it?' Bysouth asked.

'Nowhere. We shall have our picnic in the palace.'

Bysouth came into the servants' hall looking old. 'I think I've heard it all now. You are to picnic in the palace.' He went on repeating, 'Picnic in the palace.' Then suddenly his face cleared, he began to jig around and finally burst into song. 'We'll picnic in the palace, just you and I sweetheart. We'll picnic in the palace on ham and apple tart.'

We all fell around the place laughing. He was an unpredictable cove was Bysouth.

On that journey up to town Freddy, the chauffeur, had to stop for petrol as he had forgotten to fill up. He then lowered the window to pay.

'Do you want the stamps?' the attendant asked.

'What stamps?' queried Marina.

'The Greenshield stamps, of course.'

'What are Greenshield stamps?'

It was obvious that the attendant thought he was dealing with a loony, but he couldn't be sure, because loonies don't usually travel around in Rolls-Royces. So he persevered.

'Well, you stick them in a book and when you've filled it you can either hand it in to one of their shops and get a gift with it, or save it up, fill more books and get a better gift.'

'But I haven't got a book.'

'That's all right, I'll get you one or two.' He went into his cabin to oblige.

'It's all rather exciting, don't you think, Constance?' Marina said to her lady-in-waiting. Constance was about to reply when the attendant returned.

'Here you are, mum, there's three books and the stamps.'

'But there isn't anything that tells me what I can get when they're filled.'

'Yes, mum, there's a catalogue.'

'You don't happen to have one do you?'

The attendant was now a broken man. Without a word he went back to his cabin, got a catalogue, thrust it into the Princess's hand and made off fast.

'What a jolly little man,' she said as we drove away. 'It will give us something to read on our way to town,' she chuckled. I must have heard the story some half a dozen times at the dinner table. Even the Queen was treated to it.

Each year while we were at Coppins the two events that caused us most concern took place: Royal Ascot and Wimbledon fortnight. During Ascot week we had a full house, and had to engage outside servants, which could be dicey, as many other country houses around were having to do the same. Fortunately Buckingham Palace had a list on which we could call, and during the two years I was there, the same faces would appear. Help was needed in the kitchen, for valeting and in the dining room, and the head housemaid also demanded assistance.

Apart from the work, Ascot week could be a rewarding time for Bysouth and myself, especially if fancied horses won. We used to study the guests' faces when they returned from the meeting and could tell instantly what kind of day they had had. Even the men's carnations acted as a sort of barometer, for a drooping buttonhole indicated an empty wallet. Tips, therefore, varied with their luck.

For Bysouth, the week was a great occasion. He was a round-the-year punter, though he seldom referred to it. He always hoped that one of our guests might know of a racing certainty which would enable him to retire into quiet gentility. He was never that lucky, of course. However, he did have some good days, which would make him grow more expansive.

'Mrs Bysouth will be pleased at my good fortune,' he once remarked.

'Oh, does she approve of your having a little flutter then?' I queried.

'Approve, Peter? Approve? Mrs Bysouth doesn't know about it, and must never know.'

'Well, then, why will she be pleased if she doesn't know?'

Bysouth puffed himself out like a bullfrog. 'I am a man of principle, Peter. I believe that if I practise a small deceit on Mrs Bysouth, I must make due recompense. Therefore every time I have a good day on the horses, I buy her a present commensurate with the size of my winnings. In that way she is pleased, my conscience is clear and it makes for a happy home. If ever you get married, Peter, which I hope you will, it's a good lesson to learn for it can be applied in many ways.'

Although, like all youth down the ages confronted by their elders, I was critical of much of Bysouth's behaviour and his way of doing things, it was impossible not to like him and to appreciate what he stood for. Indeed, when I look back over my three years working under him, I liken myself to a young man of nineteen, who finds his parents stupid, bigoted and old-fashioned, and yet, when he is twenty-five, is amazed how much wisdom they have and how much he has changed over the past few years.

So Ascot came and went, to be followed shortly by Wimbledon. In a different way this caused an irritating change of routine. We didn't have guests in the house, but had to serve irregular meals. For once we could not rely on the time for either dinner or supper. It was a movable feast, depending on the state of play, for even if the final set went on seemingly for ever, the Duchess stayed there watching it. She genuinely had the tennis bug. As President of the Club, she showed an interest in every entrant. She knew the curriculum vitae of most of the players and of their friends and families. She spent as much time studying the expressions on their faces as watching the game. She made no secret of the fact that her favourite was Rod Laver, whom she would follow from court to court. She was on terms with the Club's officials, and showed particular interest in the ball boys, all of whom were recruited at that time from the Shaftesbury Homes of which she was a patron.

When she came back, even during the evening meal the television would be on, and she would live through the high spots of the day once again. Each evening, before she left, the firm which did the catering presented her with a chocolate cake. (She must have once said how much she had enjoyed one of them.) When either Bysouth or myself opened the door to her, she would hand us this box and say to whom she wanted it given, such as the gardener's wife, one of the chauffeurs, a particular housemaid and so on. I came in for one or two to give to my mother. One evening Bysouth confided in me that all the time he'd been with her, she had never offered him one for Mrs Bysouth. I thought this was a bit unfair and said so. I promised to have a word with Her Royal Highness as I was quite sure it was something she had overlooked and would be glad to put right. He didn't object. The following evening as she began her cake routine I interrupted her and spoke of Bysouth's omission.

'No,' she said, 'I want this to go to the head housemaid.'

I must have looked a bit taken aback.

'You know, Peter, I think Bysouth gets enough out of me one way or another.' With that she smiled and glided into the drawing room.

Bysouth, of course, knew what I was going to do and when the hoped-for cake didn't find its way into his hands, he wanted to know why. This put me in a quandary, and it showed.

'Come on, Peter, let me know the worst.'

Before I told him I said he wasn't going to like it but it only made him the more curious, so out it stumbled. It's easy to guess what he called her, though harder to describe the expression that came over his face. I did succeed in softening the blow a bit, but the rest of that Wimbledon he refused to open the door to her and, although he carried out his duties to the letter, his manner was frosty to say the least.

If we found Wimbledon a trial, so much more did Miss Arter, for if Marina was fond of tennis, she was equally fond of the opportunity it gave her for dressing up. It fell on Miss Arter to satisfy her royal in this way. Miss Arter would clutter about like a hen with its chicks, but I think she enjoyed herself as much as Her Royal Highness did. This was her opportunity to show the world the result of her labours and she knew she had the most perfect model to display her talents. The dressmakers and milliners might believe that the responsibility was theirs, but in her eyes they only played a minor role. The total creation was Edith's. Frankly, I think everyone on the staff felt they had something to do with it, for just as we lined the hall when Marina dressed up for the ballet or the like, we did the same when she left for Wimbledon.

Of course, we all sighed with relief when we said our goodbyes. Now, at any rate, we could relax for a few hours and keep an eye on her movements every so often by turning on the television. Only once did we get caught out or, I should say, two of the housemaids got caught out. The Princess had departed, Miss Arter was taking a well-earned rest, so these two girls took the opportunity to try on a few of Marina's hats. Apparently they were gadding around, striking what they thought were elegant postures, when in walked Marina. She had forgotten something. There was nothing the housemaids could do except look bloody stupid and mumble their apologies. The Princess had no time to lambast them then and there, but they got the rough edge of her tongue when she returned that evening. As if that wasn't enough, Miss Arter laid into them. 'It was as if they were her bloody hats,' one complained to me later.

My mother holding me, three months old, at our home in Fortunegate Road, Willesden, London

RAF Hednesford, nr Cannock, winter 1952

Aged eighteen, outside my home in Alperton, Wembley, on my motorbike

Playing the part of the butler in Terence Rattigan's play, *While the Sun Shines*, during service in the RAF. I am on the far right

Shirley and I on our wedding day, September 1958

The Christmas card sent to me by Princesses Marina and Alexandra in 1956

Right The Duke of Kent as a teenager
Below Princess Alexandra at her piano,
watched by her mother

Princess Alexandra, Madame
Poplewska-Koziell (Madame 'Pop')
and another European princess
taking tea in the garden at Coppins

Arrival at Liverpool Street station
from Sandringham: myself, Princess
Marina, Princess Alexandra and the
Duke of Kent just visible

The Baroness de-Stoeckl, my next door neighbour at the cottage at Coppins

The Christmas card sent by the Queen and Prince Philip to Princess Marina in 1957. Taking down cards after Christmas that year, I'd asked Marina if I could keep this one. 'Yes Peter, of course', she'd replied

Top Bear Place,
Twyford, Berkshire, my
first butler's position in
1958 working for Lord
and Lady Remnant

Middle Coppins; a view
of the playroom and
music room

Right Washing-up after
the Queen Mother called
for tea in 1962

Above left Signed
photograph of Alice and
Henry, Duke and Duchess
of Gloucester, given to me
on leaving their service

Above Signed wedding
photograph of the Duke
and Duchess of Kent, 1961

Left Christmas card sent to
the Kents from the
Gloucesters. This found its
way to my pantry and was
thus added to my
collection

At the front door of
Bear Place in 1966
when visiting.

The Duke and Duchess
of Kent and the Earl
of St Andrews
photographed while in
Hong Kong

Shirley and I leaving home for Princess Alexandra's wedding in 1963
The drawing room at Coppins in the fifties

FIVE

So, I continued happily with the Princess and her family. There were many laughs, and I felt I was learning all the time. I listened hard and made notes, particularly about areas which interested me. Food was one of these and so were the experiences of other butlers. I was fortunate that Bentley, Princess Alice's butler, who lived next door, was a mine of information. His source was a chap called Gabriel Tschumi, who had been an apprentice chef with Queen Victoria only a couple of years before she died, but he had heard her discussed by those who had been with her a long time. Not that there was much talking in the kitchens, all the chefs were kept too busy. I became fascinated by Bentley's accounts of kitchen life in Tschumi's day.

The staff at Buckingham Palace when Tschumi joined consisted of over 300 indoor servants, and there was a kitchen staff of forty-five. There were even Indian cooks who prepared curries every day, whether or nor they were wanted. The old Queen was by then very frail, but the image of her as a severe woman after the death of Albert was false. She was quick, gay and enjoyed life to the full. Her severe image was only reflected in her photographs and her dealings with politicians. It was an indication of Queen Victoria's care for her staff that, when Tschumi's mother died, he was given an audience; the Queen tactfully allowed him to speak of his grief, which may have made him feel a little better.

Sometimes, when the court moved to the various houses he would not be included in the party. Instead he would work in the kitchens of some bigger London hotels to broaden his experience. Excellent though the cuisine was, he found that it did not compare with that of the Palace. This was an age when people didn't 'eat to live', they 'lived to eat', and the Queen was no exception, though her appetite was not what it had been. This did not stop her from providing a sumptuous table for any guests. In 1900, for example, dinner was:

SOUPS
Consommé de faisans aux quenelles
Purée de choux-fleurs

FISH
Cabillaud aux œufs
Merlan frit

ENTRÉES
Mousse de jambon aux concombres
Pojarski de volaille

RELEVE
Bœuf rôti, choux braisés
Noix de veau Bouquetière

RÔTI
Dinde farcie

ENTREMETS
Haricots verts sautés
Choux de Bruxelles à l'anglaise

SWEET
Bombe glacée au chocolat

SAVOURY
Croûtes de sardines

SIDE TABLE
Hot and cold Scotch fowls
Tongue
Beef
Salads

It doesn't need much imagination to appreciate the amount of work that went into preparing a meal like this, and they were a frequent occurrence. The ultimate responsibility fell on Monsieur Menager, who would examine each dish at various stages of preparation and deliver his verdict. He took any blame there was, but generally he received praise from all sides and from people of every country.

Bentley had details of the banquet for Victoria's Diamond Jubilee in 1897. Twenty-four extra French chefs were specially brought over. The most important dish was *rosettes de saumon au rubis* (cold salmon with claret jelly). This was left to one of the French chefs. The first salmon was over-cooked and lost its colour, so could not be used. At the second try all went well until the *rosettes* came for final inspection. The claret jelly had not been prepared properly, but the chef thought he could get away with it. Menager would not be fobbed off. Eventually the required result was achieved, but not without some harsh words.

As some indication of the amount of food needed, it was not unusual on important occasions for 200 legs of mutton and 200 shoulders of lamb to be sent in one delivery. Then there were pheasants, partridge, quail, plover, woodcock and snipe. Often 200 pheasants would be used for one meal. It was enough to set the hearts of nature conservationists beating double time today. There would, of course, be loads of fruit and vegetables, prawns, oysters, Italian truffles and hothouse grapes grown at Windsor for garnishing. A regular dish was quail stuffed with foie gras, garnished with oysters, truffles, prawns, mushrooms, tomatoes and croquettes. In addition there was deer and venison, and Welsh lamb, which was thought to be the tenderest in the country. Considering that dinner and luncheon were full-scale meals, it was surprising that breakfast too, was such a size. There were chops, cutlets, steaks, bloaters, sausages, chickens and woodcock, trout, turbot, snipe, and a variety of egg dishes. The Queen was always up for breakfast, but towards the end of her life she didn't eat a full meal. Bentley was told that whenever there was a visit from the German Emperor, who died in 1882, he was to be given his favourite dish. This was a turkey, stuffed with a chicken, which was stuffed with a pheasant, which was stuffed with a woodcock. The whole was made into a pie and served cold. I reckon that that takes some beating for sheer extravagance.

Garden-party menus make today's offerings seem spartan. Tschumi had a major hand in one in 1900 when the card read:

Les sandwiches de bœuf
Les sandwiches de jambon
Les sandwiches de poulet
Les sandwiches de langue

Les gelées de Macédoine, fruits au champagne
Les bavaroises au chocolat
Les bavaroises à la vanille
Les compôtes de fraises à la Bordelaise

Les pâtisseries assorties
Le plum cake

Les glaces de fraises à l'eau
Le café glacé
Limonade

Claret cup. Hock cup
Les fruits assortis

Five thousand guests were there. To cope with the voracious appetites of the time, an extra three helpings per person were held in readiness. Nobody could grumble that there wasn't enough to go round.

After the death of Victoria and the period of mourning which followed, there was over the whole Palace an air of brightness, which sprang from the new royal couple and Queen Alexandra in particular. Every morning she visited the kitchens and showed great interest in all aspects of the menus, questioning the chefs on how the dishes were prepared. She was therefore very popular and it was also good for discipline, with all the staff wearing spotless uniforms and working at double the pace until she had finished her rounds.

With the new reign there was a lot of shuffling of staff. Some were laid off, others thought it was time to make a change. Tschumi decided that he would stay. Although Manager was a hard task-master, he was very fair, and there was still a lot to learn at his hands. As Bentley remarked, this kind of loyalty does not go unrewarded, and the two men

grew close, with Tschumi benefiting from any perks that
were going.

The next major event, and one which had some disastrous
unforeseen consequences, was the banquet in June 1902 for
the Coronation. Two hundred and fifty guests were to be
present and the dishes had to be extra special. There were
2000 quails, 200 legs of mutton and many other foodstuffs,
including sturgeon, foie gras, caviare and asparagus. The
main fish course was sole with five different sauces, and for
dessert liqueur jellies and a strawberry dish of such intricacy
that it took three days to prepare. Extra staff were again
needed, never a happy mixture, and since the day-by-day
preparation of normal meals had to continue, most of the
work was done in the evenings, often well into the night.
Practically everything was ready the night before, and they
were working on the final preparations for the great day.
Then came the announcement that the King, who had been
very poorly, had worsened, and that the Coronation would
have to be postponed. This took the staff by surprise; it was
an eventuality no one had foreseen. What were they to do
with all the food? Some of it could be kept in ice boxes, but
most would perish. The jellies were melted down and put into
champagne magnums. Over 250 bottles were thus filled.
There were still many exotic dishes which had to be disposed
of. These were given to an East End charity to be shared out
among the poor families of the area, who must have wondered at such bounty bestowed upon them, and who must
have thought much of the food peculiar anyway.

Shooting parties were very much a part of the royal life,
beginning at Balmoral in October, with guests from Windsor
Castle. Sandringham was the scene for the main event of the
year, grouse shooting. The season opened on 9 November,
the Queen's birthday, and continued for four weeks. The
ladies would lunch from hampers; about thirty-six were
needed. It was Tschumi's job to prepare this lunch and to
unpack it. There would be such dishes as mulligatawny soup,

Scotch broth, venison, stewed mutton, game pies, Irish stew and finally plum pudding and apple farci. According to Bentley, the presents at Christmas were more generous than they were in my day. There were for every employee a brace of pheasant and a haunch of venison, though this was given twice a year, not just the once. In addition there were articles of silverware.

Later in his service Tschumi prepared breakfast for the royals. The menu read:

Petites soles frites
Haddock à l'Anglaise
Œufs en cocotte
Œufs pochés
Bacon á l'anglaise
Poulets grillés au diable
Bécassine sur canapés
Les viandes froides à la gelée

The King liked to make a full breakfast, particularly if he was going on a day's shooting.

The hamper lunch for Royal Ascot was even more sumptuous. You can imagine the preparation in the serving of such a meal as this:

Consommé froid

Mousse de crabe, sauce rémoulade
Filets de saumon à l'Isabelle
Chaudfroid de volaille à la Christiana
Noisettes d'agneau nappées à la Valenciennes
Jambonneaux à la Montranches
Cailles froides à la Bohemienne

Asperges en branches froides

Eton mess aux cerises
Gooseberry fool. Pâtisseries à la Parisienne
Biscuits glacés aux pêches
Mignardises

BUFFET
Derby beef
Agneau, sauce menthe
Bœuf rôti. Bœuf pressé
Galantine de volaille. Langue à l'écarlate
Jambon d'York. Pâté de poulets
Poulets à la gelée

Salade de Romaine

Gâteaux de pain bis. Tarte de groseilles
Babas aux liqueurs

Local dishes were served on particular occasions. Pigeon pie for dinner on Ascot night. Turtle soup and whitebait on Derby night. Lunches of shrimps and lobster when at Cowes, haggis at Balmoral, with deer pudding as a savoury.

Tschumi was with Queen Alexandra on a Mediterranean cruise on the yacht, *Victoria and Albert*, when they heard that King Edward was seriously ill. The royal party travelled at full speed to Venice, whence they returned to England by train, arriving just before the King died on 6 May 1910.

There were many changes in staff. Monsieur Menager made way for Monsieur Henri Cedard, and Tschumi became his assistant. Queen Mary saw to it that the tradition of Edward was maintained. King George's private menus were dominated by relatively workaday dishes like Irish stew, cottage pies, cutlets, game pies and roast beef – food he had become accustomed to while in the Navy. Curry and Bombay duck had to be served at every meal, and sweets were apple charlotte, apple dumplings, or apple tart, plum pudding and pancakes.

Queen Mary, in contrast, liked many of the richer dishes, so two menus had to be prepared each day. Official dinners were still served as lavishly as before.

With the declaration of the First World War, there were drastic changes, which could never have been foreseen. There were now to be only three courses to each meal, nothing could be cooked in wine or sherry, and no wine served at the table, just water. Entertaining was limited only to those concerned with the running of the war. To top everything, Queen Mary sent a message to the kitchen that meat was to be served only three times a week. This apparently caused a deal of trouble with the royal children, and they would sneak down to the kitchen to scavenge what they could. Queen Mary caught them at it, and they never did so again. The Duke of Gloucester was the only exception. He claimed an extra egg for health reasons and got away with it.

In October 1915 Tschumi and Monsieur Cedard accompanied King George on his first visit to the Western Front. Two lorries were provided to take the stocks of food, but it was discovered that much could be got on the spot. King Edward's hot box came in most useful when they were travelling. The Prince of Wales was also present at the Front. He was twenty-one at the time. Then came the news that the King had had an accident. Immediately it was thought that he had been wounded or might even be dying. The Prince of Wales then arrived with the King, who had been thrown from his horse. Two doctors, Sir Bertram Dawson and Sir Anthony Bowley, quickly arrived and the party returned to England in early November. There was another visit to the Front between 1916 and 1917.

Because meat could not be served at lunchtime, omelettes, scrambled eggs, rice and asparagus were the royal fare, while the staff made do with vegetable pie till it was coming out of their ears. The end of the war was like the relief of Mafeking.

When President Wilson was in this country at Christmas 1918 a huge banquet, almost like the old days, was laid on. The menu was:

Consommé de tortue
Rosettes de truite Wellington
Cailles épicuriennes

Jambon froid à la Windsor
Filets de poulet de printemps à la crème
Asperges, sauce mousseline
Bombe Waterloo
Fraises Saint George
Friandises
Paillettes au parmesan

King George had a regular breakfast: five days a week he had egg, streaky bacon and either sole, trout or plaice. At weekends he had sausages as well, but when Yarmouth bloaters were in season he had these in place of the sausages.

Towards the end of 1928, the King became unwell and underwent an operation. Tschumi had to provide special invalid dishes, for the King had lost a lot of weight. He prepared menus which, it was hoped, would persuade His Majesty to eat. Beef jelly was the most nourishing of all. Then the King went on to vegetables, *œuf cardinal* with chopped lobster, and every evening he had an egg flip with brandy. He eventually left the Palace for Bognor Regis, where the sea air did wonders for his appetite, and he was soon eating chicken, egg and turkey dishes, and stewed fruit. Little and often was the watchword from then on until his death in January 1936.

In 1932 there was a national crisis, which was matched with a cut in the expenditure by the royal family. It was decided that those servants who were past their prime and who had been in service longest must go, and a hundred or so were made redundant. No redundancy payments were made. So much for recognition of service. Among them was Tschumi, who, although he was by no means among the older ones, because of his early apprenticeship had then the longest unbroken time with the family. He did not retire, but went to Welbeck Abbey as head chef for the Duke of Portland, and since Princess Alice was a constant visitor, he was able to keep in touch with Bentley.

During the Second World War, Queen Mary went to Badminton, home of the Duke of Beaufort, but she had her summer holidays at Sandringham. Tschumi was asked to stand in as chef there for one period. In 1947 he was offered the job as Queen Mary's chef at Marlborough House. He began his new duties on 1 January 1948. Most of the servants were of the older type, which made things easier for him. The kitchen staff was small: a cook, three kitchen maids, and a scullery maid. By now there were certain modern labour-savers like refrigerators and gas stoves. Like Marina, the Queen agreed the menu for two or three days in advance.

Queen Mary was fortunate in her friends, for she received food parcels and game, which helped eke out the rations. Every June the Aga Khan sent a box of mangoes. One year there was a card which said 'My love' and this found its way to the kitchen. Tschumi and the staff took it to mean the horse which the Aga Khan had entered in the Derby and they all duly had a good bet on the nag of that name. Great was the excitement and rejoicing when it came home.

The Queen was like a watchdog over her family and their children. Let one prince ask for two slices of cake, and that would be given from then on. It was the same with her daughter or sons. She found out what their favourite meal was, lunches and dinners, and it was given to them regularly. Such were the limitations of her imagination. The Duke of Windsor liked haddock or *œufs en cocotte* with strong coffee for breakfast, a little salmon for lunch, and for dinner oysters, grouse or game and a savoury.

Queen Mary was fond of sweet things and there was always a large box of Floris chocolates in her sitting room too. She was also particularly fond of desserts, especially a dish called 'Rod grod'. This was made of currants, raspberries, sugar, water, Danish sago flour and potato flour. She didn't care for root vegetables or salads, except lettuce. For the main course she liked asparagus, ham, fish or chicken.

She was particularly generous towards the staff at Christmas and she chose the gifts herself, which, considering there were still 120 of them, was no mean feat. A special lunch was also given the servants on her birthday and on those of George V and George VI. There was also whisky for the senior servants and beer for the others.

Queen Mary's love of the theatre was well known and after the performances there would be supper parties with up to ten guests. There were breaks in the summer and at Christmas for visits to Sandringham. Unlike the other members of the royal family past and present, Queen Mary didn't go in for pets. She believed that dogs should be kept for shooting and live outside.

Tschumi's health began to fail. He was now seventy and on doctor's orders was told he must retire. He did so some five months before Queen Mary's death in 1953. So ended an outstanding career in royal service.

There are many stories and various snippets of folklore concerning different servants and households. Let me begin with Gordon Grimett, who in 1915 went as lampboy to Longleat, the Marquis of Bath's home. What exactly a lampboy was Gordon couldn't discover, though he inquired widely before he joined. He found that the Marquis didn't approve of electricity or gas. It was felt that to install either would mutilate the ceilings and walls and the characters of the rooms would change. He had the same feelings about central heating. It was all right for the foreign aristocracy, they were a soft lot, which was why the British Empire was there and would always remain there. It was also the reason why Gordon had to collect, clean, trim and fill 400 lamps. This was not always humanly possible, and from time to time the odd-man, the steward's room boy or the hall boy would be sent to help. Officially the lamps were entirely Gordon's responsibility. Collecting and replacing them meant a good few miles' walk every day. They came in all shapes and sizes, many of them of great beauty and value, gathered from all parts of the world.

As if this wasn't enough, he was also candle boy. There was a service each day and the chapel was lit by 140 candles. He also had to lay out the vicar's cassock and surplice and help him into it, and finally sharpen his quill pen. Extinguishing the candles was the worst job. Gordon used a taper on the end of a stick, which was supposed to stop them smelling, but it didn't and the stench pervaded the place. When the candles had burnt down to within two inches, they had to be replaced. These candle ends were his perks and he sold them to the local grocer for so much a dozen, thus earning an extra couple of quid over the year.

As an example of the sexual restraint that servants were expected to observe, there was quite a furore when a nursery maid and the groom of the chambers announced their intention of getting married. The house was in an uproar, both above and below stairs. How could they have met, let alone been together for the length of time necessary to allow acquaintance to ripen into affection? A full-scale inquiry was launched, and the children gave the game away. The lover's tryst had been over the nursery sink. Not the ideal place for romance, but beggars, or domestic staff at any rate, could not be choosers. They had to leave, of course; otherwise heaven knows what the children might have seen or heard.

Powdering is something that has vanished from the domestic scene and I was mighty glad that it has, judging from what I heard about it. Gordon had occasionally to use it at Longleat. There was a special powder room for the footman. They would troop in and, with towels round their shoulders, dowse their hair with water, lather it with soap, comb it out and then take turns in sprinkling each other with violet powder. Great care was necessary as it was considered a grave offence if any powder was seen on a livery jacket.

Matching footmen were another species. Again Gordon, who was exactly six foot, was occasionally asked to go to Arlington House for state luncheons. All he and his equally tall fellow did was to stand in the beautifully lit corridor without moving. It wasn't easy since, as the powder dried, it seemed to drag the hair from its roots and the scalp itched like mad. However he appreciated the opportunity to observe the glitter and glamour.

When he was footman to Lady Astor, Gordon attended on the guests arriving at a large reception for the Rhodes scholars. It was dry; no alcoholic drink was served in that well-known teetotal establishment. This meant that the lavatories were in constant use by those who had come with hip flasks. A brash American came in a little late with a peer of the realm on his heels. He handed in his coat, hat and a gold-knobbed cane, saying to Gordon, 'Look after that stick of mine, it's kinda fragile.'

'It looks robust enough to me,' said the peer.

'Take a look at that,' said the American, unscrewing the top and withdrawing a long glass tub containing an amber-coloured liquid. 'There's a pint of rye in there. Comes in real useful in these prohibition days in the States. It should come in useful tonight too.'

He winked at Gordon, who responded with a stony sort of stare, the stock-in-trade of a good foootman.

It was a nasty, cold November night and a little later, turning to his colleague, Gordon said, 'Are you thinking what I'm thinking?'

The colleague was. He walked over and got the gold-tipped cane, and the two of them finished the lot within five minutes.

Some time later the owner of the cane appeared, waving his cloakroom ticket. 'Just the cane,' he said, and went into the lavatory, only to return seconds later.

'What the hell's going on around here? Where's my rye?'

'What rye, sir?' Gordon inquired.

'That rye whisky that was in here. You saw me showing it to that old geyser when I arrived.'

'That may account for it,' Gordon replied. 'Yes, a gentle-man did come down and ask to see the cane. He took it to the lavatory to show some friends. I thought you knew him so I gave it to him.'

The American looked as if he would explode. 'Give me my hat and coat, I'm off. If this is British hospitality, I've had it!'

The moment he was out of earshot, Gordon called out, 'No, it was American hospitality, and *we've* had it.'

Lady Astor had a seaside home, Rest Harrow, at Sandwich in Kent. It was a civilized house and her ladyship found plenty to amuse her while she was there. There was one romantic occasion that Gordon Grimett recalls. 'One morning, Mr Lee [the butler] sent for me and told me that her Ladyship had loaned Rest Harrow to Lady Louise Mountbatten, Princess of Battenberg. She was to spend her honeymoon there with Gustavus Adolphus, Crown Prince of Sweden.' Mr Lee had told him that the honeymoon was secret; he would join Gordon later and they would attend on the royal couple during the two weeks they would be in residence. Gordon did a bit of research before he left and discovered that Lady Louise was thirty-four and the Crown Prince forty-nine. 'They left it a bit late,' he thought, and comforted himself with, 'Perhaps they'll be making up for lost time, so there won't be too much for us to do.'

The happy couple arrived in what he later learned was a specially built Daimler with a high body, which had been selected because the Prince was six feet tall. Gordon blanched a bit when he jack-knifed out of the car. He hadn't seen the bridal bed but it seemed to him that the Prince was likely to have some uncomfortable nights. Mr Lee was there and quickly took over. Travelling with their Royal Highnesses were Mr Neillson, the Prince's valet, who knew no English, and Lady Louise's personal maid. Gordon asked Mr Lee how he should address the royal couple.

'Your first greeting in the morning will be "Good morning, your Royal Highness," and if you have cause to speak to them further, it will be "Sir" or "Madam".'

That night dinner was served just for the two honeymooners. They conversed in whispers with the occasional giggle. Hovering outside the dining room was the resident

Rest Harrow housekeeper, Mrs Avery. 'Whispering Avery' the under-staff called her, on account of her habit of putting her mouth up against your ear when she had something she thought important to say, and when she'd finished, bringing her elbow smartly into your ribs as if to say, 'Just between you and me, eh?' Since she did it with all the staff, it seemed she was full of open secrets.

'How many hot water bottles shall I place in the royal bed?' she asked Mr Lee.

'I'm afraid I don't know, and I've no intention of hazarding a guess,' he replied. 'I suggest you ask Lady Louise's maid.'

'I've done that and she said that up till now she always had three.'

'Under the circumstances, I suggest that tonight one will be sufficient,' said Mr Lee with great authority, though how he arrived at that figure is impossible to conjecture.

Mrs Avery seemed satisfied and, giving Mr Lee her customary dig in the ribs, she retired.

Another character who has disappeared from the social scene is the linkman. His job was to stand outside the front door with a lantern to control the flow of traffic as the guests arrived and to call up the carriages or cars as they left. While a party was on he would go round checking and memorizing where the various vehicles were parked. Then he would retire to the nearest pub and wait for the guests to come out. The routine would be for the footman announcing the departing visitors to shout, 'Lord So-and-so's carriage.'

'Lord' Edwin Lee of Clivedon was the title given to perhaps the most famous son, born in 1886, of Ellesmere in Shropshire. His father died when he was very young and he went to work for his uncle for meagre wages. They didn't get on so he left, went into service as a third footman, worked his way up and before the First World War was valet to Lord Astor. As valet he had to shave his employer, and since he was only given two days' notice of this new task, he practised on all the men servants. He enlisted in the war, and was eventually discharged with the rank of company sergeant major and returned to the Astors. With the death of Lord Astor's father immediately after the war, his son had to surrender his seat in Parliament. Lady Astor took over from him, winning the seat at the next election, and was the first woman to sit in the House of Commons.

In 1920 the butler, Parr, was given the sack and Lee was appointed to take the job. He had several brushes with Labour Members of Parliament. There was the case of Mr Will Thorn, who refused to 'masquerade', as he called it. This was all right in theory, but took some courage in practice, and with growing qualms Thorn watched the bedecked guests entering the ballroom. Eventually he decided to take the bull by the horns and enter himself. Lee was announcing that evening and Gordon Grimett was passing him the names. He had just announced a distinguished member of the peerage and his string of decorations and appointments, when he piped Gordon with 'Mr William Thorn,' then, dropping his voice to a stage whisper, continued, 'Turned-down collar, coloured shirt with tie, blue suit, cut-away short jacket.' Lee just managed to get Mr Thorn's name out before he had to flee to the lavatory, roaring with laughter. It happened that the press got the story and Will Thorn heard about it. He took it in good part and often told it against himself.

There was a very famous occasion when Lady Astor was behaving particularly badly in front of guests. Lee found it too much.

'I'm sorry, my Lady, I seem no longer to be able to please you, so I must give in my notice,' he said.

'Your notice, Lee?' Eyes began to twinkle.

'Yes, my Lady, I'm off.' He turned to go and she ran towards him.

'In that case, Lee, you must tell me where you are going, because I'm coming with you.'

After Lord Astor's death in 1952, Lee continued to serve Lord Billy, his son, eventually leaving to retire in 1963. It was a year before the Profumo scandal. Lee's comment on this was that Lord Billy was tried, judged and found guilty by the public on no evidence at all, and people used him as a scapegoat for their own misdemeanours, whether they were in thought, word or deed.

Charles Dean was another country boy who, after serving in the army during the First World War and surviving the Battle of Ypres in 1915, became a batman. When he was discharged he applied for a job as second footman to the Duke of Beaufort at Badminton, where during a season there was hunting five days a week, and coursing and shooting on others. The house was constantly full of guests but there were enough staff to cope with them. His Grace the Duke was a great character, both mentally and physically; he weighed twenty-four stone (nearly 350 pounds). His hunting days were over by then, but he followed the horses in an old open Ford, a Tin Lizzy as they were called. Its seats had been removed so that, sitting in his Windsor chair, the Duke could be hoisted into the back by the footmen and lashed in. Off he would go, shouting and swearing at the chauffeur and giving hunting cries, for all the world as if he were still part of the field. Unsuspecting guests who were not riding would be invited to follow him in their Daimlers and Rollses. The Ford had a high clearance and could go up rough farm tracks or even across ploughed fields, often leading his followers to their doom.

Unfortunately the Duke was incontinent. Opportunity would have been a great thing, but of course once strapped in the car he couldn't get out and as may be imagined it wasn't pleasant for the footmen when, after a day's hunting, the Duke had to be carried upstairs; two poles were inserted in slots in the Windsor chair and they lifted him four at a time. Invariably Charles got the rear end and the odour that went with it. He got some wry comfort from the thought that the valet had it worse than he did. He had to use a block and tackle to lift his Grace in and out of the bath.

Edward, Prince of Wales, was a frequent visitor to Badminton. Apparently he was a bit of a nuisance to them all. He wasn't a good rider, more off than on, and since he was heir to the throne, everyone was scared for his life, except the Prince himself, who was a game young cove.

Jimmy Weedon was another of the great characters at that house. He was titled under-butler at Badminton but he did a bit of everything. He had gone there forty years before as telegraph boy. It was in the days before the telephone and he was there to take and transmit messages in Morse code. He stayed on. He was three parts blind and did everything by place and touch. He also did part duty as lampboy and, as such, was a family showpiece. He would collect the lamps in front of the guests in the sitting room, then take them behind a screen and, as he poured oil in, would tap the sides of the lamp. Often a guest would inquire about the tapping, and the Duchess would say, 'Oh, that's Jimmy doing my lamps. He's blind, you know, but he can tell how much oil is needed by the sound they make when he taps them.'

In the spring of 1925 Charles Dean moved on as butler/valet to Prince and Princess Obolensky. They belonged to the fast set who, when the war was over, went around forgetting it in their own particular way – parties, drinking, dances, night clubs and so forth. It lasted until the General Strike of 1926. Being night birds, they slept until eleven every morning, which put the work of the whole house back some hours.

Charles liked the Prince, for although he was impecunious he was a pleasure to serve. The Princess was one of the richest heiresses in Britain. Although their home was Hanover Lodge in Regent's Park, it was home in name only. After the London season in midsummer, they left for the States, staying first at Newport for the sailing, and then going to Rheinbeck in the autumn. They returned to London for Christmas and then in January left for St Moritz for the skiing, then on to

the Ritz, Paris, and later to the South of France, where they
stayed at the Carlton in Cannes. They returned to London
after the spring as the new season began.

Charles crossed the Atlantic twenty-eight times with the
Obolenskys on ships like the *Majestic*, *Olympic*, *Berengaria*,
Mauritania, *Aquitania* and the *Leviathan*, always travelling
first class. Packing and knowing what was where was a great
art. The couple travelled with ninety-nine pieces, most of
which were trunks. Getting through customs was also an art,
but it didn't always work. Once, on arrival at New York
harbour with a great stack of trunks gathered all around him,
Charles was approached by a customs official.

'Jeez, is all this yours?'

Charles explained who he was and who the luggage
belonged to.

The official was not impressed. 'I don't care if you're butler
to Antony and Cleopatra, you're going to have to open
some of them. We'll start with that one.' He pointed to a
trunk containing the Princess's riding clothes. Charles
opened it and the customs man rummaged around a bit and
came out with a pair of riding breeches.

'What are these, your lady's passion killers?' He then
pulled out some other bits and pieces.

'They're her riding habits,' Charles spluttered.

'Riding habits? It seems to me that your Princess has some
very nasty habits. You can pack up this trunk and then
perhaps we can have a look at your master's dresses.'

By 1931 the Princess found that the title and her affection
for Obolensky had worn thin, so she decided on a divorce.
Charles had watched the marriage decay but he remembered
his training – 'Hear no evil, see no evil, speak no evil.' For him
those three monkeys set a good example. He found that the
hanky-panky of the rich was much the same as that of the
poor, so 'what the butler saw' was similar to what everyone
else had seen.

In December 1932 the divorce came through and early in

1933 his mistress married Raimond von Hofmannsthal. He was the son of the Austrian Hugo, the librettist for Richard Strauss. Charles was able to relinquish his valeting duties to an Austrian, Max, who acted as chauffeur/valet.

Charles learned a deal about wine through his association with his new master, who early on in the marriage bought part of the Rothschild cellar when it was put up for auction. He took great pains in matching the wines to the food. A frequent visitor to Hanover Lodge was André Simon and they would spend hours together discussing the various vintages. Charles was able to listen to them and to extend his knowledge when he superintended dinners given by the London livery companies, at which he was often asked to assist.

Once again he saw a marriage decay. This time it was quicker, and by 1937 his mistress had obtained another divorce. He was interested on whom her choice would fall on the next occasion. When he heard, he realized that his time in service with her had come to an end. As he says, he was not a snob, but the idea of being in the employ of an ex-editor of the *Daily Worker*, the communist newspaper now called the *Morning Star*, was not one he was prepared to consider.

When he gave in his notice feathers began to fly. It seemed that for the Princess changing butlers was more upsetting than changing husbands. He was offered more money, then Alice Astor's agents sent for him, trying flattery and offering still more cash. Finally, and this he thought took the biscuit, von Hofmannsthal asked him to go and see him.

'Please stay with her, Dean. She'll need you more than ever now.' He still stood fast.

When he went to say goodbye, she tried her final card and burst into tears. Charles tells this story not to boast, but to show the dependence people had on servants who had been with them for any length of time.

He then worked for the Bouveries, who had a house in Regent's Park, almost next door to Hanover Lodge. The garden was six acres. It even had a bothy, a kind of dormitory-cum-living and eating quarters for the gardeners, of whom there were seven, with a woman to prepare their food.

Mrs Bouverie was a close friend of the royal family, particularly the King and Queen and the Duke and Duchess of Kent. Her mother, Mrs Willie James, was perhaps the most famous, or notorious, of Edward VII's mistresses. I can't resist quoting here a poem that Charles told me concerning Mrs Willie James. I don't know who wrote it but it is, I think, apposite.

There will be bridge and booze till after three
And, after that, a lot of them will grope
Along the corridors in *robes de nuit*,
Pyjamas, or some other kind of dope.
A sturdy matron will be sent to cope
With Lord — who isn't quite the thing,
And give his wife the leisure to elope,
And Mrs James will entertain the King!
Prince, Father Vaughan will entertain the Pope,
And you will entertain the Jews at Tring,
And I will entertain the larger hope,
And Mrs James will entertain the King.

One weekend, just after Charles had joined the staff, the Duke of Kent arrived without his valet, John Hall (who later became his batman and was killed in the same aircrash as the Duke). Charles was therefore called upon to act as valet for the Duke. He and the Duke got on so well that the Duke gave John time off whenever he visited the Bouveries, and whenever Charles went to Coppins, as he often did, particularly during Ascot week, John arranged to take a holiday, telling the Duke that Charles would be a more than adequate substitute. His Royal Highness must have been of the same mind because one of Charles's most treasured possessions was a cigarette case given him by the Duke and inscribed 'George and Marina'.

With the outbreak of the Second World War, the Bouveries decided to sit it out. They were fortunate that there was a natural air-raid shelter in the garden, a sort of cave which was furnished, with heat and light installed. There was even a drinks cabinet. The King and Queen occasionally shared it with them, and the servants. It wasn't possible for staff to get closer to the royal family than being in the action with them.

Eventually the house was hit by a bomb and the Bouveries moved to Julians, a glorified farmhouse near Baldock. Again Charles watched another marriage going on the rocks and again he stayed with the lady. As a flower-seller he once knew in New York said to him, 'These ladies you serve seem to change husbands regularly, but never butlers.'

Charles was called up in 1942. He was discharged early and after a succession of jobs was asked if he would take on the post of butler to Lord Harlech, the British ambassador to the United States. He agreed immediately. During his life in service he had come to regard the States as his second home. He loved the country and the people. He knew that these days only in an embassy could he perform the skills he had learned. Entertaining would be on the grand scale, and tax-payers' money would always be available to pay for it. He enjoyed the work, renewed friendships and made others. When the six months of his appointment were up, he was looking forward to returning home, but he reckoned without Sir Patrick Dean, the new ambassador, whom he described as one of the greatest gentlemen it had been his privilege to meet. So he soldiered on. He was there when Princess Alexandra visited America, and he superintended a dinner party of 110 guests. Eventually he returned home on the QE2, just in time for the shooting season.

Charles's trouble, he said, was that he kept his hair and that it remained jet black, so no one would believe that he was growing old. As he approached eighty he began to look in the mirror regularly. At last he saw what he wanted, his first grey hair. 'That's it,' he said to himself. 'I'm finished. Now I can tell them that the old grey mare ain't what she used to be.' He died early in 1980.

George Washington was not christened with that name, but he adopted it from his first employment. After a few meanderings, he was appointed as steward's boy at Holland House, Kensington, the home of the Earl and Countess of Ilchester. The house was in fact run only for Mary, the Dowager Countess of Ilchester, for her son spent little time there. He had two country homes where he preferred to stay.

Holland House has a fascinating history. Almost all the outstanding men and women of genius and talent of the early nineteenth century passed through its rooms, or wandered along the many walks, and for three hundred years the plotting and planning that went on there showed results in the Parliament of Westminster a couple of miles to the east.

A steward's boy was responsible for looking after and valeting for the butler as a servant, but George was given many other tasks. Mary, the Dowager, was the widow of the fifth Earl. She was an invalid and had been widowed for many years. There was a staff of twenty-eight. One of George's duties was to wheel the Countess round the gardens in fine weather. She chattered away and he was able to learn something of the history of the house.

As hall boy he had his perks, including the empty wine bottles and corks when the young Lord Ilchester gave a dinner party. These had a second-hand value, twopence or threepence for a dozen bottles. Corks could bring in much more. All the wines served were vintage, and had the year and origin stamped on the corks. An exceptional year for champagnes, clarets and ports could fetch as much as 5s. a piece. They were resold to villains who put them into cheap bottles with forged labels, or to wine waiters at expensive hotels and restaurants. Wine waiters were expected to put the corks of the bottles at the side for the host to see, so a tipsy host paid vintage prices for cheap wine. I wonder if such trade goes on today.

After three and a half years at Holland House, George decided there was no future there for him. He joined the staff of a great lady and became associated with a fine family, the Sassoons. He was impressed, particularly with the strength of their family ties. Sir Philip, whose house in Park Lane was renowned for its beauty and its wonderful parties, and Sir Victor were constant visitors.

For the first and last time he did box work, which was a hangover from the days of horses and carriages. Instead of sitting beside the coachman, he sat next to the chauffeur in livery covered by a military-style coat in winter and a light alpaca one in summer. He also wore a cap and white gloves. He always tried wearing his cap at an angle, thinking it gave him a kind of sang-froid. Her ladyship didn't agree. She would tap on the glass partition of the Rolls and say, 'George, please adjust your cap, it's crooked.'

Another first happened to him while he was there, a visit to Lady Malcolm's servants' ball, which was held annually between the wars at the Albert Hall. It was a sort of two-way charity, the proceeds of the sale of tickets to the employers were given to charity, and charity was visited on the servants when they were presented with the tickets. There were girls a-plenty. Inhibitions went to the wind, with Hyde Park as a sort of garden where dances could be sat out. There was usually a number of servant girls who were regretting their employers' generosity a few months later.

George left to gain further experience, ending up as first footman to the Trees of Dytchly Park, Oxfordshire. There was a well-trained and happy staff, and the person who breathed her spirit into the house was Mrs Nancy Tree, who was a kind of patrician bohemian. Everyone adored her, perhaps the men more than the women. Mr Ronald Tree was a Member of Parliament and, to George's mind, the perfect partner for her, although eventually, after George had left them, the marriage ended in divorce. While they were together they kept fourteen hunters and a pair of high steppers which Mrs Tree would drive in her phaeton.

It was there that George learned how to clean hunting gear. If a coat came back filthy dirty, he would put it on a clothes hanger with two largish stones in the pockets, plunge it into a rainwater butt, leave it to soak for a couple of minutes, then hang it above the butt and brush it down with a large dandy brush. The process was repeated several times until the dirt was completely removed and the water ran clean from the jacket. He would then remove the stones, hang the jacket outside until it had drained sufficiently, and put it in the drying room, where it would drip and slowly dry. It had to be examined every so often because if it became the slightest bit creased it would stay that way. The jacket couldn't be worn the next day, of course, so gentlemen who hunted regularly would bring two. White breeches he would wash in Lux soap flakes. The chamois would be treated with a cloth ball or, if it was white, sprinkled with a yellow powder, then beaten with a little stick until the surplus dust was removed, otherwise it would fall onto the boots.

In November 1940 a top-level decision was made in London that was to affect the lives of all employed in the house. It was decided that Dytchly Park would become Winston Churchill's home and political headquarters at weekends. George and the staff were sworn to secrecy. The great man was to arrive on the Friday and by then everything had to be ready, not only for Mr and Mrs Churchill, but for his personal staff and any visitors who might call over the weekend. There was also a contingent of soldiers from the Oxfordshire and Buckinghamshire Light Infantry to act as guard. They were not to know who or what they were guarding. They were driven around in buses fitted with blinds which were drawn before they finally arrived at Dytchly. These visits became routine. Often it was George's job to valet for the Prime Minister. Churchill would arrive at five o'clock, have a cup of tea or a whisky, and go to his bedroom, get undressed and into a nightgown, the long sort that came down around his ankles, and he would sleep until eight, when it was time for George to dress him for dinner. Whisky was Winston's main tipple. The house smelt of his cigars, but he used them more as a symbol than as a smoke.

After dinner the men would assemble in the library where they would talk the night away. They were visited by the top brass of the services and the Cabinet. It was good to see these very important people looking quite ordinary as they hung about waiting for an audience with the most important person of all.

Another butler, Peter Whiteley, who was well known in his trade, was, after his early training, appointed as footman at Luton Hoo, home of Sir Harold and Lady Zia Wernher. The Wernhers were very popular with the royals: the Queen and Prince Philip went three times while Peter was there, always for a weekend on their wedding anniversary. The Queen's visit used to cause the most flutterings in the dove cotes. They were 'quite informal'. Heaven knows what they would have had to do had they been 'formal'. Peter says that the extraordinary thing was that, the moment the Queen arrived, it did become informal. She seemed to breathe her spirit into the house and everyone immediately relaxed. She was friendly without being patronizing.

I think she would have enjoyed as much as Peter did an event that occurred on her first visit there. It was a foggy afternoon and her arrival was delayed. Lookouts were posted down the drive to keep the house informed so that the royal standard could be struck the moment her car came into sight. They were all standing ready at their posts. Peter felt a thrill of anticipation as the flag went up. There was a few seconds' pause and then the Luton laundry van appeared out of the mist!

Peter had always heard that the royal family never tipped. This was not so. After each visit he was handed an envelope containing a pound. From the other servants he heard that the amount varied according to status. He knew his name was written in the Queen's hand for he checked it by comparing it with the visitors' book.

Now I must relate a story about the temptations of drink in a butler's life, which has been called 'the butler's complaint'. Someone who must remain nameless had two very big houses, which he was running with untrained or half-trained staff, some of whom were foreigners unused to our ways and with idiosyncrasies of their own. This butler began to come under considerable strain and took what he thought was an easy way out. When he felt particularly tired he would pour a nip of spirits to get him through the next part of the day. It helped, but one nip led to two and so on, until his tiredness and irritation actually became a result of his drinking. Things happened fast after that and this chap was unable to get himself under control. Inevitably it came to the notice of his employers. He expected to be dismissed, but his mistress listened to his story, told him it was a sickness and that together they would see it through. She paid for him to be treated by the highest doctor of his kind in the land. It meant many visits and subsequent weeks of torture. His work suffered, but she didn't mind, and when he was pronounced cured, she was as happy as a mother would be for her child. He hasn't had a drink since, nor do I think it likely that he ever will.

SIX

In many ways the Kents were like any other family, though perhaps circumstances made them closer than most. There was only a small group with whom they could mix. When I went there in 1955 Edward was twenty, Alexandra nineteen and Michael thirteen. Edward was at Sandhurst, Michael at Eton, and Alexandra had returned from finishing school in France.

When the three children were home together, the house buzzed. There would be a succession of dinner parties, encouraged by the Princess, who would have her meal on these occasions in her sitting room. At these and at other informal get-togethers, nicknames flashed. Michael was 'Mow' and Alexandra 'Puddy'; they also had one for the Princess – 'Min'. His mother never used the one for Edward; he was always 'Ed'.

Edward was already feeling the importance of his position. Once or twice he would get edgy and shout at me about some missing garment or mislaid trinket, but on the whole he was tidy and generally easy to cope with. If he lost his temper, he would usually apologize, unlike most royals. Marina heard him railing on one occasion and gave him a proper dressing down, telling him that for the next week he would have to look after himself. In the end I took pity on him and carried on as normal. He was fond of his food, but contented himself with straightforward menus.

Edward was as impeccable as his tailor and shirt and shoemaker could assist him to be. He was generous with clothes that he tired of, and would offer them to me, particularly his pullovers and ties.

Michael was a different kettle of fish from his brother – untidy, inclined to leave his clothes lying around. The Princess was aware of this and constantly criticized him for his sloppiness. She would make him go to his room and set it to rights. Michael was also unpunctual, but nothing Marina could say or do would change this habit. He was a pleasant lad, though, and well aware of his winning ways. I think he relied on his charm to get away with murder.

I was responsible for his clothes. At fourteen, he tended to grow out of things rather than wear them out. I would make a list of what I thought he needed, then the Princess and I would go over them. The old clothes would be taken to the village by the Princess's maid and disposed of through some charity.

Alexandra returned from France with one obsession. She wanted to be a nurse. Now that was fine, except that in a short time she would have to undertake official duties. She was adamant, so a compromise was reached: she went to Great Ormond Street Hospital for two or three days a week. She enjoyed it, but it was obvious that she could not embark on this permanently and that royal duties came first. She acquired her first lady-in-waiting in 1954. Lady Moira Hamilton, daughter of the Duke and Duchess of Abercorn, was even taller and quite a bit older than Alexandra. She was relied upon for guidance and advice and shared many of Alexandra's interests. Also in 1954 Alexandra first headed the court circular as patron of the Junior Red Cross when she visited their headquarters in Grosvenor Crescent.

Although scholastically she was not top class, Alexandra was an excellent pianist. Bysouth would frequently berate me for hanging about when she was playing. It would be anything from jazz to the more obscure classics and most days she would spend an hour and a half practising, much to Bysouth's annoyance. 'Not my kind of music,' he would say, and clatter about while she was playing. Then he would break into some ballad to show us what his kind of music was.

In those days Alexandra looked like a plump version of her mother. Her figure worried her and she believed fruit would help, so she devoured it like an animal, again to Bysouth's displeasure. She grew up fast, as girls of that age do: the puppy fat melted away and she blossomed into a youthful replica of her mother. When she was eighteen she was given a lady's maid as a birthday present. Sounds peculiar, but it's true. The maid's name was Marjory Dawson.

One of Alexandra's characteristics, and one that charmed me, was the way she would sing out 'Good morning'. I really felt that it heralded a good day, and although I never required her assistance, some of the women servants told me that she was concerned about them; if they had any problems she would listen and always do her best to help.

Of course, she was learning to become supremely dress conscious like the Princess, and I was told by Marjory that at times her mother would ask her to be present when she dressed so that Alexandra could see why certain things had been chosen for particular occasions, especially the hats.

Among the younger guests when I first started at the palace were Prince Charles and Princess Anne. They were seven and five respectively, and Charles brought his violin and Anne her hoop. He seemed a serious child; it was as if he was already feeling the responsibilities that would later be his. Having been welcomed by the Princess, he played his piece for 'our' children, then disappeared to Bysouth's pantry where he handed the instrument to Perkins, the detective who went everywhere with him. It then fell to me to take him upstairs to the children's old playroom, which had been laid out for the occasion. As Charles grew older, he didn't seem to alter – he was always a serious young boy. One of the first

things that Perkins said to me was to be sure that any ornaments of value were carefully put away, as Anne was as wild
and as uncontrollable as a young colt. Considering the way
her interests have developed, that could not have been a more
apt observation.

Perkins was a jolly sort of chap. He drank tea and wouldn't
be persuaded to take anything stronger, though Bysouth
offered it. He didn't talk about his job; it would have been
bad form.

This was the first of a number of visits from the Buckingham Palace children. The young Gloucesters were also visitors, subdued and politer versions of the boys I was later to
get to know well.

For our young people there were parties to concerts and
the theatre. Tickets for shows were booked in my name so
that there would be no fuss, unless the youngsters were
recognized by the press. That way I became well known to
box offices in London theatres, especially the Haymarket which
often staged the kind of comedies they enjoyed so much.

It is difficult to recall the names of all their various friends.
Jane Sheffield was one. She later married Jocelyn Stevens,
editor of *Queen*. There were also Robin and Fiona Douglas
Home, and Alexandra's cousin Elizabeth of Yugoslavia, but
the list was longer. These young people were all very polite to
the servants. It was amusing to see them fumbling in their
pockets as they left as though they were going to tip either
Bysouth or myself, then saying lamely, 'I'm a bit short at the
moment. I'll make it up next time, eh?' Like tomorrow, next
time never came. I sometimes said, 'Look, if you're a bit
short, I can lend you a bob or two.' It was a bit unfair and
sent the blood rushing to their cheeks.

One occasion I shall always remember was Prince
Edward's twenty-first birthday in October 1956. It gave me
great pleasure to take him his breakfast and greet him with,
'Good morning, your Royal Highness.' Until he reached the
age of majority, he was merely 'Prince Edward'. Even at that

hour he thought it a great joke and thanked me for remembering. Apart from the title, it didn't make much difference to him, though officially he was now the head of the family and, I believe, came into some money which his father had left in trust for him.

His birthday celebrations caused the staff a lot of extra work, but it was family and so well worthwhile. The first function – an official luncheon – began disastrously. Somehow three newspaper reporters managed to slip into the palace. They split up and began chatting up the guests. Her Royal Highness eventually spotted them and they were somewhat roughly removed. Things didn't stop there though. Buckingham Palace was informed and for once moved fast and furiously. All editors were told what had happened and were informed in no uncertain terms that if such a thing occurred again, all facilities would be withdrawn. An undertaking was demanded that this kind of behaviour would never be repeated and to the best of my knowledge it never was.

For the next two parties we moved lock, stock and barrel to Coppins. To my surprise, the first was for us, the servants. It was a buffet lunch, with food provided by outside caterers. Wives were also invited and there was one royal to each of the nine tables. I had Princess Alexandra at my table, which pleased me no end, since it meant that conversation would be a lot easier. There weren't any speeches.

We had clubbed together and brought Prince Edward a silver salver, suitably inscribed. I say we – there was one refusal, the odd-man. 'I'm buggered if I'm giving some money for a piece of silver which I'm more than likely going to have to clean when you're not around, Peter. I reckon you must all be out of your bloody minds.' His sentiments didn't prevent him from enjoying the food and drink. Lunch over, we all had to change back into our working clothes, but everyone was of the opinion that it had been worthwhile and was delighted that the staff had been remembered.

The main party three days later at Coppins was again a buffet do, with the full treatment – lobsters, whole salmon, game pies, you name it. For once we even had strawberries out of season. Again, it looked as though events were against us. During the preparations, when we rolled back the carpet for the dancing, we discovered that the parquet flooring had swollen and was so uneven that it would be impossible to use. Emergency measures were put into action: a sanding machine levelled the floor in a matter of hours, much to everyone's relief, particularly Princess Alexandra, who had been near to tears. The majority of the guests were her friends. The Joe Loss Band provided the music. He was always popular with the royals. Everyone behaved impeccably and I noticed no drunken behaviour when I helped serve breakfast around 3.30.

The only clanger of the evening was dropped by yours truly. It was one o'clock in the morning. I'd had a couple of drinks with our pretty young kitchen maid, so to the distant strains of the band we took ourselves as partners for a dance, jigging and jiving round the servants' hall. The door opened and in walked the Queen and Prince Philip. The kitchen maid and I separated. We needn't have worried, both their Majesties were wreathed in smiles.

'Sorry to interrupt, but the Queen and I were looking for Mrs Keeble, your cook. We have met her at other houses, you know, and we just wanted to say hello.'

I was able to tell him that Mrs Keeble had retired to bed about an hour ago.

'Oh, well, please be sure to convey our very good wishes, won't you? In the meantime, I suggest you carry on enjoying yourselves,' and the Duke's eyes twinkled as he ushered Her Majesty out.

Prince Philip was in those days a very down-to-earth person and sometimes he would make excuses for things going wrong. On one occasion, on a hot summer's day, he brought his mother, Princess Alice, dressed as usual in the habit of her religious order, to lunch at Coppins. Marina decided it would be pleasant to have lunch on a glass-topped table in the garden. After the main course of fillet steak had been cleared, I went to the kitchen to collect an ice cream bombe, strawberry-flavoured and decorated around the base with fresh strawberries from the garden. Alas, as I approached the table, which was quite near a wallflower-lined herbacious border, I tripped and the bombe toppled over straight onto the wallflowers. The ice cream had started to melt, so it did not take much effort to displace it.

Marina, looking serious at the disaster, changed her expression as she saw her cousin Philip beaming.

'Oh well, never mind,' he said. 'I'm sure we have had enough to eat.'

Bysouth, who was watching, looked as serious as Marina did, but on returning to the pantry he commented, 'Well, I knew he would pass it over like that.'

A major part of my job, of course, concerned food and the serving of it. At Coppins breakfast was taken in the dining room, but at Kensington Palace everyone had breakfast trays in their own rooms. Marina's tray contained more silver than anyone else's. Silver milk jug, coffee pot, toast rack, cereal bowl. This latter had a flat silver lid on which other food could go, and another cover on top. There was also the inevitable pencil and notebook on which each morning were written the menus for the next few days for family, guests and staff. The main breakfast was cereal, followed by brown toast and a selection of thick and thin marmalades, each in a silver container. Coffee, ready ground, was sent from Fortnum and Mason's and occasionally the Princess might have a croissant. She had her own silver crested napkin ring with the letter 'M' on it, and the napkin and tray cloth also carried her crest.

It was strange that one so meticulous should not consult the chefs. She seemed to avoid them like the plague. They would come and go without her knowing. Only very rarely did she ask to see one, Christmas being an exception. The family menus were written on one side of the notebook, and food for the staff on the opposite page. If she thought we were being given too much shepherd's pie or mince, she would suggest a change. She would know, if we were down for, say, cabinet pudding and she was to get marmalade tart, to reverse the dishes. Her inspection of the menus was rigorous.

Generally lunch was a very simple meal, clear consommé followed by a casserole, steak and kidney pie or fillet steak, with boiled potatoes, broccoli spears, asparagus tips and perhaps baby brussels. There was always a wide selection of cheeses from a shop in Kensington or Fortnum's. Greek cheeses were very popular. There was one in particular which looked revolting to me, like a large sausage, green on the outside and red on the inside. The foreign guests seemed to enjoy it. If wine was taken it was generally French or German. If there were several Greek guests we provided retsina and ouzo, both of which were described by Bysouth as 'pigswill'.

An idiosyncrasy of the Princess's was that she rarely sat at the end of the table; that way she felt she could talk to more of her guests, the only exception being when the Queen or the Queen Mother came and she would then adopt the formal arrangement.

Afternoon tea was at 4.30, a simple little meal with toast, croissants or crumpets. There was a silver kettle with a methylated lamp underneath. Sometimes she gave instructions, 'Just a cup of tea today.' Dinner was generally much the same as lunch. If there were guests the starter would be something like fresh asparagus, then fish, sole, salmon or lobster, usually followed by a roast or game, pudding, a savoury, dessert or cheese, with a range of wines to go with them.

A full party would need extra staff and Bysouth would ring Buckingham Palace to see if they had anyone on their books whom they could recommend. If not, we hired extra staff from a reputable agency. That way I heard many interesting stories of bygone days. Most of the agency staff had retired and just came out to exercise their old skills and for the companionship. On these occasions Bysouth was generous with the drink, but not until the work was finished, and the trays ready for the morning. The cook or the chef, however, would be given his tipple two or three times during the preparation of the meal; that way Bysouth said the chef was in such good spirits you got the full flavour. It was an example that I was later to follow. For a party there was always a seating plan in the hall which the Princess carefully supervised herself to make sure that friends were surrounded by friends. Names were also set round the table. The visitors' book was open but guests were only expected to enter their names once. King Olav was an exception. He signed it every time he came.

A tradition which has been passed down about conversation, not only in the dining room but at any time or at any place, was that there were four things it was considered bad form to mention, on which hostesses frowned and thought of as being conversation-stoppers. They were money, illness, children and the servants. Servants, of course, no longer pose a problem, but if it wasn't for the first three, there would be little but silence, even in middle-class homes, and if it wasn't for television, the silence would be complete today. Chefs, it seemed, didn't come into the category of servants, for their excellence was often remarked upon and so were the dishes they prepared. I never heard one criticized, for to have done so would have put the hostess's good taste in question.

Things did go wrong though. Chefs are temperamental and are often a law unto themselves. Occasionally, particularly if there was only one chef, his outbursts could be covered up. It happened with us at a particularly awkward luncheon party at Kensington Palace. The guests of honour were presumably Sir Winston and Lady Churchill, as he was to sit on Marina's right and she on her left, but there were sundry other notables. I was supervising the door and the drinks and Bysouth was keeping a watching brief over the food and the dining room. The invitation had been 12.30 for one and all the guests had arrived except the Churchills. As the witching hour approached, I saw Marina's eyes glancing towards the hall clock, like Cinderella's fairy godmother. One o'clock came and went, so did five past.

I felt a tap on my shoulder. It was Bysouth.

'Haven't the buggers arrived yet?' he whispered.

I shook my head.

'I've got a crisis on my hands. Chef has prepared a soufflé and he insists on serving it immediately, otherwise it will be ruined. I told him to try and delay it. He says he can't and threatens to walk out.'

I took a look in the kitchen on my way. The soufflé was a disaster, flat as a pancake. Chef was in tears and Bysouth calming him down.

'Pâté, that's the answer. There's some in the fridge, but it shouldn't be eaten direct from the cold. Peter, you stop them going into the dining room for five minutes. When Churchill arrives, be ready with a glass of whisky or brandy whether he wants it or not.'

At that moment our tardy guests arrived and I obeyed instructions. The chef recovered and the rest of the meal went without a hitch. I did see, though, Marina making a note on her pad, and I knew the non-appearance of the soufflé did not pass unobserved.

At the end of the meal, Lady Churchill remarked on the excellence of the pâté. 'Did you buy it or did you make it here?'

'We made it here, my lady,' Bysouth said, lying in his teeth (it had come from Fortnum and Mason), and without pausing for a second, 'It's one of the chef's specialities.'

Bysouth was, of course, later questioned as to why the intended soufflé had not been served. Without involving the chef he explained that the Churchills' lateness had ruined it.

He was then congratulated on his presence of mind. 'Three cheers for Lady Churchill,' was his comment to the staff.

When I had recovered from the earlier excitement, I was interested to know how the conversation would go around the table. Of course, Sir Winston was the centrepiece. Would he, I wondered, talk about affairs of state? In fact, politics didn't get a mention. He knew of the Princess's interest in art and all the talk was about that. When Her Royal Highness told him she was going to visit some friends and relations in Europe, and she hoped to get the opportunity to do some painting, he immediately offered to lend her his easel. Naturally, the Princess accepted graciously, but when it arrived, it turned out to be a heavy wooden thing, completely unsuitable for taking by air. I wondered what she would do with it. I would never have known but for once Miss Arter opened up.

'She wrote a letter of thanks, told a whopping great fib, and locked the easel in her wardrobe. When she got back, she wrote again to Sir Winston, told another fib about how helpful it had been, and returned the thing personally.'

An art, if you can call it that, that most of the royals had in common was that of mimicry. So had some of the servants. I, for one, fancied myself at it and indulged in it frequently; to a lesser extent Bysouth did the same, a little more self-consciously, perhaps. With the royals it is very understandable. They are in almost daily contact with the pompous, the self-important, the pretentious and the plain fawning, who lay themselves open to be sent up solid. They have to treat such people with tolerance, even flatter them, when more ordinary mortals would show them the contempt they so often deserve. It must be tiring and frustrating. It is not surprising, therefore, that when they return home to relax, to assume a sense of proportion, they give in to the temptation to ape them. And what was sauce for the drawing-room geese, was also sauce for the staff ganders. As far as we were concerned, no guests were sacred, neither were our em-

ployers. But we were a little astonished one day. Bysouth and
I had a first-class row, a real up and downer, which ended in
my calling him a brainless, bald-headed coot. As I
approached the drawing room, the door was slightly ajar,
and I heard Marina mimicking to her guests what she must
have just heard. She was greeted with peals of laughter which
broke off as I entered the room, though I could hear some
stifled noises from some of the younger members of the
family. When I told Bysouth about it, it helped to heal the
breach. 'We must be more important in their eyes than I
previously thought,' he commented.

One favourite they loved to imitate was Cecil Beaton,
Marina's photographer, with his floppy hat and affected
manner. He behaved towards her as a producer might to an
actress. I know he adored her, not just because of her looks
(he said she was the finest model he had ever worked with),
but as a great and gracious lady and a brilliant hostess.

It was while I was with Marina that the Margaret–Peter
Townsend business broke. He was particularly popular
among all the servants and everyone was on the young
couple's side. We thought that both of them would have the
courage to see the affair through, but it was asking a lot of
Margaret, with all the forces assembled against her. So much
has been written on the subject, including Townsend's book,
that there is little that I can add, and I don't think that history
will be able to say any more. I was in on the preparations for
the wedding to Lord Snowdon, but not on the break-up there.
My former colleagues have told me that they felt it was
doomed from the start, not so much because of anything she
did, but because he would not give up the idea of being a
photographer. When he should have been at her side, he was
following his old profession. That, in my opinion, was a
mistake.

The same nearly happened with Angus Ogilvy and
Alexandra some years later. He continued to work and was
involved in some deals in Rhodesia which attracted criticism

and were described by the then Prime Minister, Edward Heath, as the unacceptable face of capitalism. This put the cat among the pigeons, with Buckingham Palace rushing around trying to put matters to rights and pretending that Ogilvy was just a figurehead. This only made things worse. Still, Ogilvy, with a greater breadth of experience, took stock of the situation and realized where he had gone wrong. Probably he was advised by the Palace and so played along the royal route. It boils down to that Biblical saying, 'Thou canst not serve God and man.'

The year 1957 had its special moments for me. One was a conversation I had with Miss Marilyn Monroe. She phoned one afternoon when the Princess was resting and Philip Hay was out. I didn't recognize her voice, but when she announced herself I had a vision of her at the other end. It wasn't a particularly pleasant exchange. She asked whom she was speaking to and I informed her I was the Princess's butler. She obviously didn't rate that highly, judging by the tone of her voice, and asked to be put through to Marina. That, I explained, was not possible, but I promised to get a message through to her private secretary. If she didn't rate butlers, she rated private secretaries even lower. I think she had a picture of some typist and she intimated as much. I tried explaining Philip Hay's importance, and how if she gave me a message, he would ring back on his return. Realizing she wouldn't get very far with her present attitude, she softened a bit and told me that she was hoping that the Princess would honour the opening night of her new film with her presence. I promised to pass on the request, and we parted company. I found myself sweating somewhat, though whether it was having concluded a difficult conversation or from the vision I had throughout, I wasn't sure. As it turned out, Marina was unable or unwilling to attend the film premiere.

Later in the year Princess Nicholas, Marina's mother, died in Athens. She was seventy-five. Her death affected Marina deeply. The light under her portrait in the hall of the palace was turned off and instructions were given that it must never again be lit. Her Royal Highness went into deep mourning. It grieved her that she had not been with her mother at the end, but her death was unexpected, even though she had been in rather poor health for some time.

On a brighter note, Princess Alexandra had her twenty-first birthday later in the year. It was much the same as the party given for her brother but without the first official luncheon or the servants' get-together. There was one slight hitch. We had to engage extra men for help. One of our regulars was unable to come but he recommended someone to take his place. He seemed a keen enough old chap, and was obviously very experienced at these sort of occasions. I did catch him taking a glass of champagne, but took no notice. It was common practice at these dos for servants to keep their strength up with the occasional tipple. The party gathered momentum and the calls for drinks came louder and more frequent, so no one had a chance to keep an eye on what the others were doing. When we began serving breakfast, it became obvious we were short-handed, but again, with eggs and bacon coming at us fast, we hadn't time to look for the absentee. It was, of course, the stranger, and when it came for him and the other contract servants to return to London, a search party was enlisted by Bysouth. The old fellow was eventually discovered in the servants' bathroom, spark out in the bath, snoring his head off. He was as drunk as a lord. We were tempted to turn on the taps and give him the soaking he deserved, but Bysouth had a different idea.

'Get his hat and coat and put them on a chair here, then shut the door and leave him.'

'But aren't you going to say or do anything?' we inquired.

'No,' Bysouth said. 'When he wakes up he can find his own way home.'

The following day I saw Bysouth's point when he handed me five bob. 'That's your share of our drunken friend's money, Peter. He wasn't fit to claim it. I'm sure we shan't be hearing from him and since we did the extra work, I see no reason to enlighten Philip Hay and have to return his wages to him. I trust you're of the same opinion.'

I was, naturally.

The other important event in 1957, and one which was to influence the rest of my life, was my meeting the girl I was to marry. It was one of those chance occasions of which there had been a number in my life, but what was extraordinary about this one was that it almost immediately made a deep impression on both of us.

What is it, I wonder, that eventually makes a man want something more from his life than he's been getting? Of course, love plays its part, but there was something more than the hearts and flowers of sentimental popular songs and romantic novels. I had skipped my way through life and in particular enjoyed my time with Marina. I had been carefree, fancy free and completely self-sufficient, so why did I want to change the pattern? I've never found the answer, but I shall always be glad that the decision was made by me, or for me. My wife, Shirley, finds herself in the same dilemma, though confesses that one added factor was that she wanted to have children. The phoney images which had made up my dream world some years before had been severely mauled by my experiences with a real, live and beautiful princess. No matter how glamorous the parties and people had been, they faded when I opened the solid wooden door and found a kitchen piled high with dirty plates. The sight was as bewitching as the cold potatoes which were tumbled into the pigswill by the kitchen maids, and in some ways I had developed a general cynicism about life and illusions. The Walter Mitty world that had prompted me to go into service had gone long ago and I had become something of a realist.

Ours was a mundane story of two youngsters from similar working-class backgrounds. In a way the Princess was responsible for our meeting. In August 1957 she went to visit her sister Olga, Prince Paul's wife, in Florence. She was to be gone six weeks, so during this time the members of the staff were put on board wages, which meant I was given an extra two guineas a week and could live at home. Although this rest was very welcome, most of my former friends had left the district, so boredom set in. One evening I decided to go to a dance in Wembley. I rather fancied my ability on the floor. I hadn't anyone to take as a partner, but I was no shrinking violet and was confident that I wouldn't be alone for long. I was not wrong. I picked my way into a party of what I thought to be especially pretty girls and took one off for a waltz. She was no mean performer, so we stayed together until the interval. Since there was no licence in the dance hall, I whisked her off to the nearest pub, where I found her personality as attractive as her dancing. We arranged to meet for supper the following evening, and from then on the pattern was predictable. We had both lost our fathers, but home visits were arranged, mothers and relations were introduced, everyone seemed to approve, even the neighbours. When I returned to duty, there was between us what in those days was called an understanding.

Something about the euphoria of romance certainly transmits itself to other people. I had hardly been back at Kensington Palace a few hours when I began to notice sidelong glances from my colleagues. I was certainly no lovesick Romeo, but that evening Bysouth invited me into his parlour, poured me a glass of port and began probing me about how I had spent the last six weeks. It didn't take long for my romance to be laid bare before him.

'Aha,' he exploded gleefully, 'just what I'd thought, and I've been laying the odds with some of the others, though there weren't many takers. It was written all over your face.'

He then treated me to a discourse on matrimony and how to lead a successful married life in service.

'Does your intended consider working with you in the future?'

When I told him that whatever ideas she might have, I was dead against it, he nodded in agreement.

'Seldom a good idea. Neither Mrs Bysouth nor myself have ever entertained it. How are you going to manage over accommodation?'

This was an awkward one, since it could easily have given offence.

'I've decided to look around for a butler's job with a cottage in the grounds to go with it.'

It was equivalent to my giving notice, but I needn't have worried.

'Precisely what I would have suggested. You're a bit young, but I don't anticipate that you will have any difficulty. If I can be of any help, I will. I suggest, however, Peter, that we keep this one under our hats. There is no need for any of the others to know until you're suited.'

That ended our conversation, and although I was teased and questioned by the rest of the staff, Bysouth didn't refer to the matter again for some considerable time. I left him that night more conscious than ever that I had been fortunate in working under such an understanding man, and I found it easy to forgive the occasions when his pomposity and rigid attention to detail had given me the screaming heebiejeebies.

I looked forward to any time I could get off, and during our Christmas break, when the Princess went to Sandringham, Shirley and I became formally engaged. Now for the first time I was able to introduce her to my colleagues at the palace and she was able to get her first glimpse of what royal service was about. She was also able to have a taste of it, for when an order was delivered from Fortnum's or Harrods I was able to half-inch a few of the goodies.

Eventually I thought it only right that the Princess was told of our engagement. She was quite charming about it, congratulated me and made the usual noises, as did the rest of the family. I also told her that I would have to leave because of the problem of accommodation. Again she understood, but I wasn't quite sure what she meant by her remark, 'What a pity. It seemed we were just getting used to each other.' She didn't inquire as to when I would be going. She seemed content that that decision was left to me. Philip Hay was of the same opinion.

It wasn't as easy to get another position as I had thought. People were now thinking in terms of married couples or au pairs, and there weren't that many situations for single-handed butlers. One lady, anxious to employ us both, said that she was sure my wife would enjoy working for them. This I found irritating.

'Madam,' I said, 'she doesn't enjoy doing her own house-work, so I'm certain she wouldn't enjoy doing yours.'

Where there were vacancies, Shirley and I found the conditions or the accommodation unsuitable. However, we persevered, and were frequent visitors to Masseys, the domestic agency where a Mrs Bates looked after us. Through the grapevine I heard that Jayne Mansfield, the American film star, who died in a dreadful accident some years later, was in England looking for an English butler. I went to the Dorchester where she was staying and made an appointment. She was tickled to death that someone from royal service had applied.

'Do I bow to you or do you bow to me, Mr Russell?' she asked.

We made an appointment for a second interview, but I'm afraid I stood her up. Shirley and I realized that with our mothers still alive we had a duty to them, so I missed the chance I had always wanted of glimpsing the Hollywood scene.

At last we found what we thought we were looking for: a job for me as a butler/valet. I had expected to have to combine these two duties. It was a delightful country home, Bear Place, Twyford in Berkshire, owned by Lord and Lady Remnant and we were to have a flat in the main house. It was agreed that I would start with the Remnants in July 1958. I notified the Princess and all those concerned that I would be leaving around the middle of May, giving us time to buy the essentials of furniture and do the dozens of other things that had to be done before the wedding. There was nothing particularly exciting about our wedding, except for us and our nearest. Like any other married couple, we were glad when it was over, and we could settle together in our own home.

SEVEN

Peter the married man was a different kettle of fish from Peter the devil-may-care bachelor. There was also my position to consider. As butler/valet I would surely be the head of the domestic household and, as I saw it then, the job seemed to have everything in its favour.

Bear Place was a typical, medium-sized country house with delightful, if formal, grounds, looked after by three gardeners. The gardens were the pride and joy of Lady Remnant, who would often spend many hours tending them herself, taking great pleasure in showing her handiwork to his Lordship when he returned from London.

Adjoining the house was a home farm which supplied our vegetables. It struck me as strange that we had to pay for these since we owned the place; I suppose it had something to do with it having to be self-supporting.

Both Shirley and I remember the day of the interview well. Although we weren't sharing the work, she was anxious to see what was to be our first home, so we had a good deal to talk about on the train back to London.

We were met by his Lordship at the station at Twyford, Buckinghamshire, at six o'clock in the evening. To our astonishment, we were shown into an old 1938 Morris 8. We later discovered that the Remnants had a Jaguar and a Sunbeam Talbot, and a chauffeur, Mr Hopwood, who, despite his

advancing years, was referred to with scant respect by all and
sundry as 'Oppy'. The fact that we were met with the Morris
was in no way a slight to us. His Lordship used it each day to
drive to the station and since he had come down from
London on the same train as us, it was only natural we should
all use it.

Our first impression of Lord Remnant, one we didn't
change a lot, was that he seemed an affable enough cove, a
product of his upbringing and antecedents. He had inherited
his title as second Baron, went to Eton and Oxford, and was
working as something in the City. We didn't exchange much
in the way of conversation on the journey from the station,
and it became obvious that our appointment was solely a
matter between his wife and us.

We were greeted by a lady wearing a floral frock and a
flowery mimosa yellow hat. It wasn't her everyday get-up,
but she too had been up to London for the day. Lady
Remnant was a stately sort of woman, with a voice that was a
bit too loud for my taste. In a way I felt it was she who should
have had a seat in the House of Lords and not her husband,
though as time passed she softened and became almost
friendly. She inquired about my experience, in particular
about the royals, and said that I would find it very different
there, much more homely, which in the two and a half years
we were there became a word I learned to suspect.

After more chat, with Shirley looking and feeling like a
spare part, her Ladyship came to what was of interest to us
both, our accommodation. It was on the second floor, near
the nursery, and was everything we had hoped for. There
were two bedrooms, a sitting room with an open log fire
overlooking the front of the house, and a bathroom. There
were scatter rugs and our furniture would fit in well. The
kitchen was well equipped. Her Ladyship offered to lend us
any other bits of furniture we needed, and she was as good as
her word. I could see that Shirley was excited about it and
that it meant that we could now get married, since I had

refused to finalize our wedding plans until we had somewhere to share together.

Once again it was suggested that Shirley might like to work
there with me, and once again I refused the offer, though a
little more politely this time. In fact, she did occasionally help
by waiting at the dinner table, for which she got 15s. a night,
but that was only if we had a large party. She had decided to
look locally for the same kind of job she had before, as a
comptometer operator, and it wasn't long before she got one,
which helped our finances considerably. My wages were to
be £8 7s. 1d. a week after deductions. I was paid every Friday
night. It was always the same. Her Ladyship never seemed to
have the odd penny so it was assumed I would settle for the
even amount. Now this may seem a petty irritation, but as
time went by it made me testy, and I began to keep a tally as
to how much was in fact owing to me.

On our return journey, however, we were cockahoop. I
had a job, Shirley was well pleased with the accommodation,
and we began making plans for our wedding. I was to begin
work in July and would have time off for the wedding, after
which Shirley would join me. Our wedding took place on
20 September 1958, my twenty-fifth birthday, and we had
our honeymoon in Devon.

By then I had settled in to my new routine. Each morning
tea was served at 7.30. I prepared it and the cook, Mrs Gleed,
took it to the Remnants' room. As they shared a bed, it was
thought only right and proper that the cook should go,
though I've never been able to see why. The old legend of
'what the butler saw', I suppose. At a quarter to eight I had to
knock on their door to make sure they were getting up. While
his Lordship was in the bathroom I would prepare his clothes
in his dressing room. He alternated with three suits, one for
two days, the second for another two days, and the third for
the odd day. The next week it would be the other way round,
so that over the course of three weeks he would have worn
each suit the same number of days. His shirts were changed

every day, and I selected three ties from which he would make a choice. He was very particular about the way he dressed, though on Saturdays and Sundays he chose his own rough and tumble.

The Remnants had three dogs. Now, it is one thing to cope with your own dog, but coping with other people's is another, particularly in the moulting season. Justifiably, I suppose, I was reprimanded at times for the hairs on his Lordship's suits. I say the reproaches were justified, but it was the devil's own job examining every inch of the cloth and, no matter how good the clothesbrush, as often as not, I was simply moving the hairs from one place to another. If only I could have broken his Lordship's habit of nursing the dogs on his knees every evening, things might have been better, but it would not have been greeted in the spirit in which it was meant, had I mentioned it. Not unnaturally his dinner jacket (and I) suffered most. One morning, shortly after his Lordship had left for the City and with her Ladyship in her room, one of the dailies came into the dressing room, and seeing what I was doing, began commiserating with me.

'I know what I'd do if I was you,' she said helpfully.

'What's that?'

'Hold on a minute and I'll show you.' She left the room and returned with the vacuum cleaner. She laid the jacket and trousers on the floor, put the vacuum cleaner in my hand and switched it on. Just at that moment the bedroom door opened, the daily shot into the passage, and her Ladyship stood there aghast. I was caught red-handed.

'Good heavens, Russell, what do you think you're doing?' she exclaimed.

'Well, your Ladyship, it seemed the only way to get these wretched hairs off. The brush seems to have worn a bit thin.'

She picked the brush up, examined it and obviously came to the conclusion that it was not as thin as my story.

'I suggest you stick to the generally accepted method,' she said testily, and stalked out of the room.

After his Lordship had been dressed, it was time for me to go downstairs to the hall where there was a huge gong. This I had to sound. The place resounded to its boom and I felt rather like the man in the J. Arthur Rank films, though I was conscious that our physiques were very different. This routine struck me as a foolish affectation. Her Ladyship had her breakfast after her husband had left for the City so the only person to be summoned was his Lordship, and I had just left him ready to walk downstairs to his meal. His breakfast was a simple affair, fish twice a week, and bacon and eggs on other days, except Sundays when it would be bacon and sausages. Immediately after breakfast I would refold *The Times* and *Financial Times*, help him into his coat, hand him his glasses, gloves and hat, open the door, and usher him into the Morris 8 which the chauffeur had driven to the front door. I knew then that I should not be bothered by him until the evening.

Her Ladyship made up for this. Hardly had I closed the front door when she was down and busying herself. Monday was the worst day: she would supervise the laundry, checking each piece as though she suspected that some of it might have disappeared. I don't think Shirley and I were under scrutiny; after all, we had our own bed linen which was open to inspection at any time. Then there was the checking of the kitchen stores; jams, marmalades, sugar and flour, down to washing-up liquids and similar cleaning things. The cook and I would have to write out a list of what was wanted, though to my astonishment they would make the selection together, doing a job that I knew by custom should be mine. When I raised the matter, I was told that cook had been there for many years and it had always been her responsibility. Apparently in his Lordship's father's day, all the servants except the butler, who had to be a married man, had been women. No one seemed to know why. I can only imagine that there had been 'goings-on' at some time when there had been a full staff, and that sort of thing was strongly frowned on in Victorian

households. There were other houses where the opposite
view was taken, for it was considered that housemaids were
fair game for the sons of the house and if the master also
wanted a bit of a change, the maids were his for the taking.

But back to the household stores. The preserves were made
by the cook, and the date and quantity carefully marked on
the labels. I had to requisition what I thought we needed but
her Ladyship would work out how long each pot should last
and, if she felt too much had been used, she would remark
that the consumption had been excessive.

Once she fixed me with her stern eyes. 'We seem to have
used twice as much marmalade as we should, Russell.'

'Well, your Ladyship, that is indeed possible. I don't know
where it could have gone to, as I don't eat any and neither
does my wife.'

I must say, on this occasion, it ended with a smile, almost
an apology. She was the same with things like washing powder. She thought such things were gimmicks and she began
putting the date on each packet. This attitude brought to
mind the kind of conversation which I'm told takes place in
gentlemen's clubs.

'The trouble with the working class is that they don't work
any more. They drink tea morning, noon and night instead of
doing their jobs. Four large scotches, Harry.'

'You're right, and until they decide to do a fair day's work
for a fair day's pay, the country will continue going downhill.
Four more large scotches, please, Harry' – and so it goes on.
Yet ask the same men for half-a-crown rise, and it's like
taking a tooth out without using an anaesthetic. For
example, even in those days the cost of living was continually
rising. When I put in my plea for a little more recognition,
10s. a week, the Remnants were both together in the drawing
room, and a hard, set expression came over their faces. I left
the room feeling like a man who has backed a horse at a
hundred to one.

To my surprise, though, I got my extra 10s. a week.

A similar episode occurred shortly afterwards when one of the dailies wanted a rise. Quite properly she asked me to speak to her Ladyship. It was part of the daily routine that at eleven o'clock her Ladyship took a cup of Bovril and a couple of plain biscuits, so I was able to use this period to gauge her mood. I bided my time in putting forward Mrs Alright's request. I thought I had struck the right moment to do so. I was wrong. Her Ladyship's attitude changed instantly.

'What do I pay her now?'

'Half a crown an hour.'

'And how much does she want?'

'Three shillings an hour.'

'Quite impossible. In any case I sometimes wonder what I pay her for. Her job is to clean the passages, but whenever I see her she appears to be leaning on the broom handles rather than sweeping.'

Here I interrupted on Mrs Alright's behalf.

Back came her Ladyship. 'It appears you're trying to take her side. The facts speak for themselves. I have recently been checking the bills from the ironmongers and it seems that we have bought more broom handles than broom heads.'

What could one say to a woman who thought and behaved like that? I tried to explain that dailies were hard to come by, but she was adamant. Mrs Alright was quite philosophical about the result. She knew that she would have no difficulty getting another job at the rate she had asked for, so she gave in her notice immediately. It was interesting that her eventual replacement was a large, heavily built woman; although I didn't bother to check, I'm sure that broom handles were even more in demand than they had been.

I began to think that there was something the matter with me, that I was making mistakes somewhere along the line. I had no illusions that I was perfect by any manner of means, but I couldn't believe that I got things completely wrong. I decided to investigate. I knew that the previous butler, Atterbury, lived nearby, so I decided to visit him. He was well on in years and though he was affable enough, he didn't commit himself. He had got what had been his goal all his life: his own home, a little house bought with his savings and those of his wife, who had helped him by working in the house when they held a large dinner, as Shirley did. The Atterburys had no children. Meeting with no success, I decided to go to Bysouth, who was anxious to know how things were going. When I told him, he was entirely on my side.

'Tradition must be observed, that's the trouble with these upper-middle classes. They want it every way, expecting a small untrained staff to behave and do the work that their grandparents had in a properly run household.'

He worked himself into quite a lather, did Bysouth, and ended our discussion by saying that, if I agreed, he would write to his Lordship and tell him so, and that he was lucky to have a well-trained butler. That I thought was going it a bit and would do nobody any good, so I gently opted out.

It seemed to me that I was trying to get my information second hand. But at last I got a first-hand opportunity to confirm my belief in myself. To my annoyance her Ladyship was continually referring to a butler by the name of Bone who served in a house where the Remnants were regular visitors. According to her Ladyship, he was the paragon of everything a butler should be: efficient in every way, he moved in and out of the dining room without being seen or heard; the plates were served and taken away without the guests knowing it. It got so that I hated the man. That summer I discovered that on certain days of the week the house where he worked was open to the public. Both Shirley and I made an early opportunity of visiting it and paid half a crown to look over the garden and have tea. It wasn't long before a man came in to serve another party. That, I thought, must be Bone. Later that afternoon, when things had been cleared away, I went up and introduced myself. When I mentioned my name, he roared with laughter.

'You don't seem any different from ordinary men.'

'What do you mean by that?' I asked.

'Well, I'm constantly being told by my master and mistress what a wonderful butler you are.' Then he went into the list of my virtues. It was similar to those my Ladyship had used about him, and I told him so. When I finished, he once more dissolved into laughter.

'This deserves a drink,' and the three of us went to his pantry.

'I shall tell them when they return that I've met you and that we've decided to swop jobs, and I shall see to it that her Ladyship is left in no doubt about the way we both feel,' I said.

Then we fell to and started putting the domestic world to rights. I was as good as my word and there was no doubt that the message went home; for the first time I saw she was embarrassed and from that day his name was not mentioned.

The Remnants had two children, a son James, and a daughter Susan. The boy had married just before I joined. They were both very charming and easy to be with. They lived more in the present, treating servants with the deference due to them. James, I think, worked with his father, so I only saw him on occasional weekends. Susan must have had a pretty hefty allowance, but she complained about the price of things. 'You can't get a lunch for under seven and sixpence and clothes are outrageously costly.' I didn't tell her that Shirley and I never spent more than 2s. for a lunch, but I couldn't help saying that Princess Marina got many things from Marks and Spencer and looked well in them.

Most weekends the Remnants entertained and on those occasions employed Shirley to wait at the table. She quite enjoyed the experience and we both appreciated the extra money she earned. There was one occasion that angered me, however. We had had a hard night with twelve to dinner. It was after midnight and we were in bed when the bell summoned me to the sitting room. I dressed hastily and on entering the sitting room was asked to get another bottle of brandy from the cellar. I gritted my teeth to stop the oaths. Why, I wondered, couldn't they have got it themselves? They must have known that I was in bed. I asked her Ladyship about it the next day and suggested that it was inconsiderate.

'But Russell, you surely didn't expect one of us to fetch a bottle. That, after all, is what you are here for.'

I gave up. What does one say to a person who thinks in that way? Another irritating habit was when we had guests staying the night. Her Ladyship would ask them what time they would like their breakfasts. That meant preparing trays as well as setting out the dining room and ringing the gong. I was sure the guests would not have minded taking their meal at the same time.

We had some charming guests, many of whom were free with their money when they left, a rarity when I worked with the royals. I suppose it was thought infra dig and that, because we were working in a royal household, we were highly paid.

Her Ladyship's brother-in-law, Major General Dewing, was one of the generous ones. Mrs Dewing and her sister were as different as chalk and cheese, and the Major General was charming, constantly making jokes. I liked his bluff, genial sort. He was fond of his tipple, as indeed was his Lordship, who chose his wine carefully and particularly enjoyed port.

Mr Cockburn, who gave his name to the port, visited us once and his Lordship thought he would test him out. He produced two decanters of the stuff, one of 1934, the other of 1937 vintage, and asked him to identify which was which. It was quite a performance. Mr Cockburn was given two glasses, which he polished carefully with a napkin. He then poured a little port into each glass and held them to the light several times, then sipped one, paused while he nibbled a biscuit, then sipped the other. He tasted each once only, then made his pronouncement. Unhappily, he was a year out, but his Lordship congratulated him on a very near miss.

The hunt met at our house once a year. I caught it twice, and it was not a pleasant experience for me. It's a very attractive sight and it's the one time I enjoy dogs, but it was my job to hand round the stirrup cups, which is all very well if you're tall, but I am 5 foot 6½ inches (I don't know how many hands that is). Even high-heeled shoes would have made little difference – I needed a pair of stilts to hand over the traditional nip. On one occasion I was passing behind a horse with my half-laden tray when he deposited his load. I just managed to avoid it, but it was a nasty moment. I was the only person, it seemed, who thought that way, for the horsemen guffawed and made bawdy remarks. It was impossible to maintain my composure and give them one of my looks, so I did the only thing possible and joined in the laughter.

His Lordship also enjoyed shooting. Apart from the usual birds, there were deer from the estate, which would wander into the garden, chewing the plants and roses. His Lordship would straightaway call for his gun. I used to hope that he would miss; being a townie, I looked on any kind of killing as murder. There was another reason in this case. When the carcase was hung, it used to stink to high heaven. The Remnants liked it crawling. I wouldn't eat it; it was as much as I could do to serve it after it had hung around for days.

Often we had jugged hare on a Saturday, and I enjoyed that, but my favourite was the huge steak and kidney pudding at which Mrs Gleed excelled. She was good at her job, but on this occasion she surpassed herself. She also cooked a wonderful raspberry pie, with short nutty crunchy pastry, and generally her puddings were quite excellent. Before we could enjoy her pie, we had to wait until the raspberries grown in the estate garden were ripe; it was the same with tomatoes.

'You know, Russell, the tomatoes are late this year. I shall really look forward to having some,' her Ladyship would say.

It exasperated me. 'Haven't you had any yet, my Lady? We've had plenty.'

'Well, you're fortunate to be able to afford them,' she retorted tartly, putting me in my place.

Such things were part of the difference from life with the royals. There, what we needed we got. Marina was careful, but – strawberries apart – she left things like this to her staff. Her income was probably less than the Remnants' and she had greater expenses.

The Remnants were a little competitive socially, though they met their match with some new friends who had entertained them, then taken them round their private zoo. I don't think her Ladyship particularly enjoyed this.

'We've got to ask them back and what have we to show them that compares?'

I was included in the discussion, which ended by verging on the ridiculous.

'We may not have any particularly uncommon animals, but we could muster quite a variety from the farm – sheep, cows, the bull, cats and these dogs – and perhaps you could catch a couple of deer to go with them, your Lordship,' I suggested.

'Yes,' he said, 'that's a good idea, and perhaps we could dress you up as an old-fashioned shepherd in a smock, and Lady Remnant could be a milkmaid.'

It was one of the few human occasions which we shared together when class and master and man were forgotten.

I think some of the skirmishes with Lady Remnant concerned the pantry floor. It wasn't a large pantry, but I was expected to apply red Cardinal to the floor every week, which was a tedious, horrible job. The kitchen floor was done by one of the dailies, the cook didn't have to raise a finger. But the same daily wasn't allowed to do mine. This gradually wore down my endurance, until finally it got me on the raw, and I stalked in to her Ladyship. She didn't see my point of view.

'Other butlers do it without complaint,' she said. 'I can't for the life of me see the hardship.'

I explained that, in my experience and that of others I had spoken to, it was not considered a butler's duty. 'Can't you compromise? Let me put some spare carpet down, then all I shall have to do is vacuum it?' I added.

She was adamant.

This got further under my wick. 'Don't you see, your Ladyship, by your attitude you're not only demeaning me, you're demeaning your household and the way it's run.'

Another thing that led to a violent disagreement concerned one of the dogs. Now, I accept that dogs will from time to time piddle on the furniture legs and I've wiped up and forgotten the event. But if there were ever a contract between servant and master, top of my list would be that no servant should be expected to clear up 'big jobs'. Most employers, anyway, would never ask staff to do it. Not so her Ladyship. Such an occurrence happened in the drawing room. I was summoned and told to get rid of it.

'That, your Ladyship, is something I am not prepared to do.'

She then rattled on her favourite theme: 'My other butlers —'

Here I interrupted. 'I don't care if the Queen did it, I'm not going to.'

'You mean you expect me to do it, is that it?'

'You must do what you think fit, your Ladyship, but I think I have made myself clear.'

It was evident from her expression that Russell was less than the dust. Without another word, I left her with her problem.

Another irritation was that on my days off, I was expected to serve breakfast, carry out my morning duties and only leave when I had laid the table for lunch. When it came to my fortnight's holiday, I told her Ladyship I was going from the Saturday to the following Monday fortnight. This didn't suit as I was getting three weekends off instead of two. Moreover we were never allowed to use the car to go into Twyford and back; on dark winter nights we had to walk home or take a taxi. We were never offered a lift, nor was money given to us to pay for our fares. These were such small things, but they annoyed me, and again I took them as indications of the esteem in which I and my office were held.

After two and a half years, I decided that the time had come for me to make a change. Some of the reasons I have explained, but there were others more immediate. His Lordship developed 'a leg' which became steadily worse and was causing him great pain. I was sorry for him, but it added greatly to my work. I had to look after him in every way, and if I caused him any pain, he would react testily and curse me as a clumsy oaf. I didn't particularly want to be a male nurse. He went into hospital for a time and his condition improved, but by then I had made my decision. Her Ladyship also had bouts of back trouble which didn't improve our relationship. It's strange that if a servant is unwell, he is told 'the best way to get better is to work it off', whereas a master immediately takes to his bed. A further reason for us was that Shirley was pregnant and wanted to be nearer her mother. We needed a bigger place where we were not so close to the family that our every move could be watched. The difficulty was to find such a position – it was not going to be easy.

At that time Princess Margaret's engagement to Anthony Armstrong-Jones was announced and that looked just the ticket. I wrote to Clarence House, asking for an interview. I was called for by Lord Alan Gordon, the Queen Mother's secretary. The first applicant to be seen was a man called Cronin, who got the job, so the rest of us were told our journey was unnecessary. Cronin was about forty-five and highly experienced – what was known as 'being in the league'. At the time he was butler to the American ambassador. Strangely he didn't stay long with Her Royal Highness. Later we heard through the grapevine that the reason the other five of us were not seen was that the Princess was late for a fitting for her wedding dress. Naturally, both Shirley and I were very disappointed.

However, as luck would have it, a short time later I heard of a vacancy as butler to the Duke of Gloucester. I went to York House in St James's, at one time the residence of the Duke of Windsor, where I was interviewed by Major Nigel Chamberlayne-Macdonald and immediately offered the job, which I accepted willingly.

I now had the task of giving in my notice to the Remnants. I decided to write to her Ladyship – the butler's equivalent of a 'Dear John' letter, I guess. At that time Lord Remnant was in hospital. Her reaction was predictable: she thought mainly of herself.

'It's going to be most inconvenient. Are you sure you want to change? His Lordship will be returning home again shortly and both of us would be glad for you to look after him.'

I said that I thought it best if they got a nurse. I could see her mentally adding up how much that would cost and once again she asked if I was sure I wouldn't change my mind. She couldn't seem to understand. Her son spoke to me and added his pleas but he understood my predicament and what the trouble was. He suggested speaking to his mother about it, but I refused the offer and said that I saw no chance of her changing, that I'd accepted the job with the Gloucesters and would be leaving in a month's time.

So ended my happiest and unhappiest days in service. I know that is a contradiction in terms, so I'll explain. They were happy because during those years I got to know and to love Shirley, and they were unhappy because of our constant conflict with her Ladyship.

My association with the family did not end completely. Some years after I left, his Lordship died. I was invited to his memorial service at St Paul's, Knightsbridge, and saw a very different Lady Remnant. Not long after, she went to live in the dower house on the estate. I decided to visit her, and again found a very different woman, kind and welcoming. She gave me tea, and even offered to cook an omelette, saying how kind it was that I had travelled so far to see her. It was as though our relationship had been of the friendliest, and I returned home feeling that I had lost someone whom I had looked on as a foe and had gained a friend.

EIGHT

When I was offered the job with the Gloucesters in 1961, I was shown over York House by the butler Mr Carter, who had worked there for some time. Carter's opening gambit was not encouraging. 'It'll take you at least three months before you're in command of the job.' I must flatter myself here by saying that it only took me one. Carter had been butler there for nine years and he felt he wanted a rest and a change. I don't think he had another place to go to. If he had, he kept his lip buttoned tight. We arranged the visit when the Duke and Duchess were out so that I was able to see their rooms. The Gloucesters used two sitting rooms. There was a waiting room for guests, called the Chinese Room, and a large dining room.

I naturally wanted to see what our own accommodation was to be. I'd been told it was ample, but when I saw it, I was aghast. It was sprawling, occupying the top floor and part of the second. Altogether there were nine rooms, and they looked as if they hadn't seen a paint brush for years. We only had furniture for four rooms, including the future nursery. I suppose, in retrospect, it was a little churlish to be daunted by the prospect of the luxury of such space.

Before leaving I spoke to the Duke's private secretary and requested that the flat be redecorated. I also asked if a new stove could be put in the kitchen as the old one must have

YORK HOUSE
ST. JAMES'S PALACE, S.W.1
WHITEHALL 4104

7th October, 1960.

Dear Russell,

Further to your interview with the Duke of
Gloucester I am pleased to be able to confirm your
appointment as Butler here to His Royal Highness.

I confirm the following details:-

1. The engagement will be for a trial period of
three months commencing on Thursday, 10th
November, at the end of which period it will
be confirmed as a permanency if satisfaction
is given. If for any reason on either side
it is desired to terminate the engagement before
the end of the trial period, one calendar month's
notice is to be given.

2. The commencing salary will be £520 a year with
the flat and free laundry up to a maximum of £12
a year.

3. Three weeks' holiday will be allowed, with full
pay and board wages, for each completed year's
service, and at the rate of one day per calendar
month for a broken period.

4. At the end of one year an annual increment will
be considered.

../..

Mr. P.J. Russell.

My letter of appointment to the Gloucesters

5.   An annual bonus of 10% of the gross annual
     salary will be paid for the <u>second</u> and
     subsequent years' service, i.e., the first
     bonus will become payable on 10th November
     1962.

6.   Livery will be provided as soon as possible,
     but in the meantime you will wear your own
     plain clothes.   You will also get one suit
     every two years.

7.   The flat will be done up.   Any subsequent
     redecoration other than maintenance must be
     carried out by yourself.

8.   It must be understood that if you wish to
     have your meals upstairs with your wife there
     is no objection, but there will always be a
     meal for you in the Steward's room and when
     the staff go on board wages you will also
     receive them.

          I hope you will be happy here and that this
     appointment will prove satisfactory in every way.

                         Yours sincerely,

                         Macdonald

                         Assistant Private Secretary
                         and Equerry to
                         H.R.H. The Duke of Gloucester

been there since Queen Victoria's day. Finally, I inquired if they had any spare rugs or carpets; ours would look like pocket handkerchiefs there. He couldn't make any decision there and then but in a few days' time came the reply, agreeing only to the redecoration and suggesting that my wife might like to visit and select the colours she wanted. When she saw the place Shirley's first reaction was the same as mine. However, she chose the four rooms which we would use and the paint, and came away contented, if not completely satisfied. She also found somewhere where the pram could be kept near the guard room.

I hadn't realized what a shindig the redecoration was to cause. Mr Amos, the Duke's valet, had heard there was a cottage going at Barnwell, the Gloucesters' country house, at Oundle, near Peterborough. He had been with the family for so long, they couldn't refuse him, so he used to travel up to town once or twice a week and had a small room to sleep in at York House. Before my arrival he had occupied part of our flat, and when he heard that the Office of Works had painted the place for us, he was a ball of fury. 'If you're here twenty years, you get nothing done for you. Yet for a newcomer, only the best will do,' he snarled. To some degree I could see his point of view. Eventually, I gained huge admiration and respect for him. He was of the old school, highly trained and skilled, and his standards brushed off onto others. He had travelled widely, but, as he said, it was no holiday, just bloody hard work in strange surroundings.

All the rooms had open fires – there was no central heating for us. We weren't worried, since I was able to appropriate any fuel we needed from the cellar. An extra expense was the heating of the kitchen stove and the electric light. Both were on meters, with us paying the bills, a little matter which I hadn't considered when agreeing to a salary of £520 a year. However, the private secretary generously agreed that they would pay for our move to the new place.

Instead of waking to the twittering of birds, we would be

roused by bells and stamping feet, as well as morning music from whatever unit was on guard duty outside York House. We were next door to the Chapel Royal, and St James's Palace was across the road, where there was a clock tower with a loud striking chime right above us.

'I only hope the baby can rest through it all,' said Shirley anxiously.

'That's all right, love, of course it will,' I assured her, knowing nothing about babies at all. Fortunately when Ian was born he seemed to thrive on noise.

We moved in on time to a smell of paint. The Office of Works must have moved fast. We used the same removal firm as I'd had for Kensington Palace and Bear Place, and the same chaps did the work.

'Another bloody palace. He's beginning to look like royalty, isn't he, Harry?' one remarked.

'Buckingham Palace next stop,' said Harry.

'Not on your nelly,' I replied. 'Too much like a factory floor and production line.'

Chance would be a fine thing.

I began my duties with some trepidation. It was the largest staff I had served on and I was in command of it. A final remark from Mr Carter had been that both the Duke and Duchess were an uncommunicative couple, which was, in a way, a consolation. On the other hand it would be difficult to tell whether they were satisfied or dissatisfied with my work. My first encounter was with Her Royal Highness, who seemed to take my abilities for granted. She was more interested in my reaction to our new quarters, and hoped that we would be comfortable and happy there. So my first impression was a favourable one and was to stay with me during my time there. When I served at table the first two days I might as well have not existed so far as the Duke was concerned. I mentioned this to Major Macdonald, his secretary, who told me he was trying to make an appointment, and had pressing worries. I left it at that, but I felt a bit of a spare part.

A couple of days later, the Duke and I did have our first meeting. He was the third son of George V. He was born in March 1900, so missed service in the First World War. He was slightly older than Her Royal Highness. She'd been born on Christmas Day 1901, the third daughter of the Duke of Buccleuch, one of the richest families in Britain. The Duke's annual income from the Privy Purse was £45,000, a goodly sum now, let alone at that time, so between them they must have done very nicely thank you. From 1945 to 1947 the Duke had been governor general of Australia and had always had an interest in the Commonwealth, though he didn't speak about it except on official occasions, when I was too busy to listen.

Our first conversation ran like this:

'Come in, Ruskin, and close the door.'

'It's Russell, your Royal Highness.'

'What's rustling? I can't hear anything.'

Then I remembered he was more than a little deaf. I raised my voice. 'My name is Russell.'

'Of course it is. We've met several times at Kensington Palace. You were there with the Duchess of Kent, weren't you?'

I don't think he would have remembered if he hadn't consulted the notes in front of him.

'Why did you leave? Dissatisfied?'

'No, your Royal Highness. My marriage made it necessary.'

He paused. 'Why?'

'There wasn't the accommodation for a married couple.'

That threw him. 'Understand your wife's pregnant. Difficult time for a woman, and for a man. Get my meaning?'

I wasn't sure exactly what he had in mind, but I wasn't entering into any discussion on that score. 'Yes, your Royal Highness.'

'Understand this is the biggest job you've had. Difficult

one, eh? Mixture of old and new staff.'

'That is something I've met with before.'

'Who have you met before?'

I raised my voice. 'It's a situation I have met before.'

'Ah, yes, a situation.'

The questions waned. I noted that by now His Royal Highness was sweating under the strain.

'Your parents still alive?'

'My mother is, my father isn't.'

'Last war casualty?'

I told a white lie. 'He died as a result of it, yes.'

'What did he serve in?'

'A Border regiment in the Army.'

'Where?'

'Mostly India.'

'Interesting, that.'

There was a long pause.

'Well, that will be all, Ruskin.'

'Russell, your Royal Highness.'

'Ah, yes, Russell, of course. We shall see a lot of you, Russell. Good morning.'

I don't know who was the most relieved, him or me. I needed a strong slurp of scotch, something I never usually took at that time of the day. It had scarcely been so much a conversation as a rather poor interrogation.

There was a large staff: the valet, two chauffeurs, for the two Rollses, three footmen, a lady's maid, cook, house-keeper, housemaids and an odd-man. We menials adopted the old-fashioned procedure when eating. In the steward's room there were myself, the valet, the lady's maid and both the chauffeurs if they were in on time. The others used the servants' hall in the charge of the housekeeper. Our meals were served by the third footman. The odd-man carried the food. The senior and junior staff mixed together in the evening, sending out for beer and often playing cards. Sometimes they were joined by members of the guard. The policeman on duty was given his supper and would join in. Everything generally went very smoothly.

I can only remember two nasty incidents. One night I was woken to hear that the policeman had seen a naked man on the roof. It was the third footman, an agency chap, called Donald. I didn't know a lot about him, he had only recently joined, but I shouted at him, 'I know it's a hot night, but don't you think you're overdoing it. Come on in.'

He didn't cause any trouble. When he had got his clothes on, I took him to the stewards' room, gave him a drop of the Duke's whisky and talked to him. He told me that he had had a nervous breakdown and had been sent to a mental home, from which he had recently escaped, and had come to us as a refuge. I arranged for him to be collected and returned to care. He hadn't been gone a week when he sent me a letter and a book, thanking me for the help I'd given him. Aptly enough the book was called *Clothes and the Man*. I have always been astonished that the agency hadn't fully checked him for security. I was able to keep the whole thing quiet, which took some doing with a staff our size.

The hiring of domestic staff by a butler is usually a function demanding a combination of many factors. An applicant's past curriculum is usually important, as employers will consider it an 'upmanship' if they engage a cook from a ducal household, say, or from someone with a title senior to their own. Comments like 'she came from Lady So-and-So or Viscountess Someone Else' are often heard. Appearance, too, is important; employers like to see smart people around them as staff frequently run into guests. One also needs to be able to talk freely with applicants to find out if they are at ease in conversation, which indicates potential for a good working relationship.

In particular if you know and respect the judgement of an applicant's previous employer you will feel confident in hiring him. If you are desperate for help and someone appears to be a good applicant but has a weak service background, you may be duped by their tales of work in various catering environments as I was when I hired Donald. It is a risk, but I think Donald was my only 'disaster'. As for dismissing staff, this rarely happens unless there is evidence of heavy pilfering or a similar misdemeanour. Reprimands are sometimes given to footmen for upsetting female staff, or for continually making mistakes while serving at table – for instance, not placing the spoon and fork at a convenient position to be picked up to allow the host, hostess or guest to transfer food to their plates, or making too much noise when opening and closing doors, or talking too loudly to other staff outside the dining-room door.

The other incident which caused me some concern was with a cook. The staff, and I agreed with them, were angry about the kind of food they were getting. It was shepherd's pie four days a week. They came to me with their complaint and asked if I could do anything about it. That evening I spoke to her. You would have thought I had called her every sort of bastard. Screaming at the top of her voice she picked up a knife from the kitchen table and made at me. Now, I'm no coward, but the sight of that woman brandishing a knife will live with me for ever. I didn't stop to reason with her but made my way to our flat in double quick time.

'Lock the door,' I panted to an astonished Shirley. 'There's a mad woman trying to kill me.'

The business of climbing the stairs brought the cook to her senses. The following day she was all penitence.

'I don't know what came over me. I'd had a couple of gins, but they've never done that to me before.' All was forgiven, though not forgotten, certainly not by me.

It was part of my contract that I would be supplied with a livery which I would wear when I was on duty. I was also allowed one new black suit every two years. The livery was similar to a military-type battledress, though of better cut and material, dark blue with gold braid on the lapels and epaulettes, and with His Royal Highness's crest and the initial 'H' on the left pocket. The footmen had the same, only their braiding was red.

Shortly after I joined, our son Ian was born at St George's Hospital, Hyde Park, not far away. The Duke and Duchess were away at the time on a visit to Turkey, which made things easier for us. He was born the day before their return, and the first thing the Duchess said was 'Are you a father?' and congratulated me. The Duke stood their grinning and said something like, 'Now your troubles will start.' He was in such a merry mood, I thought he was going to offer me a bottle of champagne to wet the baby's head. He didn't, but I 'borrowed' one anyway and a bottle of brandy to go with it, sharing it with some of the senior members of the staff. There was something special about having a baby in a royal palace. I felt almost like one of the royals myself. The difference was that the birth wasn't announced in the press, and if I had telephoned the Queen to tell her, I should have got an icy response.

Strangely enough Prince William, the Gloucesters' son who was killed in an air crash in 1972, asked if he could come and look at the baby. He seemed most intrigued, playing with him as though he were a relation. It seemed odd behaviour from one who was known as a bit of a wild boy. His father was regularly remarking on this to his face. It didn't stop Prince William, nor prevent him from teasing his father. I once overheard this exchange.

'Wouldn't you like to live permanently in London, Father?'

'You know damn well I wouldn't. I can't wait for the weekends and Barnwell.'

'But there's so much going on in town.'

'Goings on, that's all you seem to think of.'

'I say, steady, Father.'

'Well, it is going on, with your fast living, fast cars, fast friends – and fast women, I shouldn't doubt.'

'Not to mention ladies in the clubs. Oh, that reminds me. I

shall have a few people coming round later tonight. Will it be all right if we have a bottle or two of wine?'

'Ha, you're a scoundrel. Yes, you can, damn you.'

One day shortly after Ian's birth, when we had just finished serving lunch, Her Royal Highness turned to her lady's maid and asked to be reminded where they were going that afternoon.

'Well, ma'am, you're opening a baby show at the Westminster Hall.'

With that the Duke, who had been in a brown study, looked up. 'Oh, God, is someone having another bloody baby?'

The Duchess, conscious that Shirley had just given birth, tried to restrain him, but he was in full flood. 'Too many babies already.'

'Shush.'

'I won't be shushed.'

'I'm opening a baby show this afternoon.'

'Can't stand babies. Nasty, messy, noisy things.'

The Duchess gritted her teeth and whispered loudly, 'Don't you remember? Russell has just had a son.'

'Oh, my God, that was a bit of a clanger, eh? I wasn't including Russell's baby, just royal babies, eh, what?'

I could hear Prince William trying to stifle a laugh at his father's discomposure.

When Her Royal Highness returned that afternoon, she apologized for the Duke. 'He sometimes doesn't think before he speaks.' Then she told me about the baby show, and suggested that Shirley and I should go. We did, and bought a christening gown, which has been Shirley's pride and joy ever since.

The Duke was concerned about his deafness, though sometimes he would use it for his own ends. He would ask for whomever he found it easiest to talk to to be placed on his left. This meant that whoever was on his right struggled to make conversation, gave up and had to content himself with the

person on his right. At one state occasion at Buckingham
Palace there had to be one royal for each table. He was put
at one with Joshua Nkomo. 'You'll have to move me,' he
said. 'I sat next to him last year and couldn't understand a
word he spoke.' His wishes were obeyed.

Perhaps it may seem strange, considering his eccentric
habits and his often seemingly rude manner, but the Duke
and Duchess were very fond of each other. They shared the
same bed, though each of them had a separate dressing room.

The Duke wasn't an early riser. He was called at eight
o'clock, had his morning tea, then a bath, which had to be
kept at just the right heat. There was a thermometer for this
purpose. His bath in the evening was several degrees hotter,
for he had more time to wallow in it. The valet would put out
his shaving equipment, unscrewing the tops of the various
bottles and his toothpaste. There had to be a cigarette next to
every ashtray, and a matchbox in a solid silver cover with a
match jutting out so that he didn't have to open it. I never got
over the incredible privilege that these small duties represented. Call it helplessness, naivety, sheer laziness, or mere
habit, these little chores – only taking a moment to perform –
represented the huge gulf between master and servant even as
recently as the 1960s. The fact that I was prepared to accept
such conditions, and the fact that they never seemed to
consider it strange that something as exquisitely pointless as
preparing a match for their next cigarette should be done for
them, speaks volumes not only about the nature of my work
but on the whole structure of class and hierarchy.

The Duke then dressed and had his breakfast in his dressing room with the morning papers. He had several, but
always looked for and read the *Daily Mirror* first, not *The
Times* as one might have supposed. The meal was the same
every day: three rashers of bacon with the rinds and any
gristly bits cut off, and a fried egg on fried bread. The egg and
the bread had to be of the same circular shape, so the cook
would fry a square of bread, then with a serrated pastry

cutter she would cut the bread into the required round. The egg was placed on top and and also trimmed. Lunch was light and variable. He didn't seem to care too much what he ate then although he certainly had some favourite foods. Unless we had visitors, soup was never served. Sole was his favourite fish, either grilled or prepared with a sauce. Potatoes he was particular about. They all had to be of the same size and the kitchen maid spent many hours cutting them into shape. Directly a plate was placed in front of him with his crest and the initials facing towards him, he would test it for heat. If he didn't think it was warm enough, he would send it back. He could be very impatient about this. I served him first and then went round the table and served the Duchess. She sat immediately on his right and very close to counteract his deafness. He was fond of straightforward British food, and he particularly liked game, a quantity of which was sent down from the royal shoots.

Most of all he enjoyed partridges in cream. I was fascinated by this and learned how to prepare it. It is cooked in butter, with an onion chopped and sliced, two or three leaves of celery and a bay leaf. It is then placed in a large saucepan. One liqueur glass of brandy and three of chablis are added. It is then flamed to make sure of the right flavour. Chicken or game stock is then added, covering half the partridges. The whole is then cooked for about forty minutes. The partridges are cut in half and placed on a dish. The stock is reduced, and a little cream and milk added to make a sauce, not too thick. This is poured over the partridges, topped with button mushrooms already sliced and cooked in cream. Finally it is garnished with small rolls of grilled streaky bacon. Not exactly British cooking, but the Duke was nothing if not eccentric. He could afford to be.

Cheese and biscuits seemed to be his favourite course. The biscuits had to be at a certain heat. One footman had turned the hot plate off early on in the meal but the ensuing fuss ensured it was something he would never do again. The Duke felt them, then, taking one in his hand, he called the luckless footman over and put it against the servant's ear, crunching it.

'Can you hear anything?' he asked.

'No, your Royal Highness.'

'Of course you bloody well can't. They're stale, that's why. Go and get some fresh ones, and make sure they're at the proper heat, d'you understand? Bloody fool,' said the Duke and flung the bits of biscuit after him.

The cheese, like the butter, was prepared at the farm at Barnwell and was the only kind that he would eat. It came in two-ounce portions, wrapped in greaseproof paper. Sometimes it would come down with the Rolls, more often it was sent by train to King's Cross. It wasn't put in the fridge, the Duke wanted it fresh. Came the awful day when there was a train strike, I knew there would be trouble. I had the cheese board put out just in case I could persuade him to accept another kind, but I could have saved myself the bother.

'I'm afraid there isn't any of your usual cheese, your Royal Highness,' I began.

'What, no cheese?'

'There are alternatives. I've brought in the cheese board.'

'There are no alternatives, and you bloody well know it. Why isn't my cheese here?'

'There's a train strike.'

'A bloody strike. There shouldn't be strikes. What's it about?'

'The usual, your Royal Highness. The men want more money.'

'Well, why doesn't someone give it them, then I could have my cheese.'

I was reminded of the poem by A. A. Milne about the butler – 'The King told the Queen and the Queen told the dairy maid . . .'

'I bet if the Queen wanted her cheese, they'd get it for her.'

The Duchess intervened. 'But you're not the Queen, and they're hardly likely to consider your wishes.'

'Then we've got to beat them. Send Foster to Barnwell in your Rolls.'

Cheese was missed that day and he was in a black mood for the rest of the evening. The Duchess took to her sitting room immediately while His Royal Highness had an extra glass of port to compensate. He was as regular with his drinking habits as with other things. He didn't drink wine even when there were guests, but he normally had in front of him a small whisky decanter, some six inches high, with a silver lid and his coat of arms on it, together with a small port decanter. The organization of these drinks was one of my duties. I half filled a tumbler with whisky, added a little Malvern water, then put in six balls of ice. Not five, not seven, but six. After dinner came the port with his coffee. He would then go to his sitting room or join Her Royal Highness. I followed with the grog tray. The Duchess didn't drink, she seemed to thrive on Malvern water and orange squash so that was included on the tray.

As I got to know the Duchess, I realized she was a stronger character than I had originally thought. Everything had to be just so, and this wasn't merely to please the Duke. Before a dinner party she would inspect everything. She was precise, almost fussy, although she wasn't like Princess Marina. She would change the table decorations and play around with the chairs. She was, I think, a very private person. She liked reading and she seemed always to be writing letters. When they were at Barnwell, she was out as often as possible, generally alone. She was also very exact and conscious of protocol. In the presence of the Queen and any of the servants she would go through the formalities as though the two of them were poles apart. Yet privately, the Queen was Lilibet and the Duchess was Aunt Alice and the Duke Uncle Harry. The servants rarely heard such familiarities. I was of necessity an exception. It was the practice of the Queen or the Queen Mother that, when they wanted to use the loo, they informed the Duchess, who in turn told me. I then told the head housemaid, who arranged for a housemaid to stand near the door, holding a hand towel for appearance's sake. The housekeeper would tell me when all was at the ready, I would tell the Duchess, who discreetly would inform Her Majesty. On one occasion a housemaid, who should have been on duty, was undressed and ready to take a bath. She was told to put her clothes on fast. There must have been some breakdown in communications for it appeared that Her Majesty didn't want to use the loo after all. The housemaid was furious and seemed to think that it was me trying to play a joke on her. Nothing I could say would convince her, and she refused to speak to me for over a week, tossing her head whenever she met me.

An occasion when the Duchess showed a stubborn side to her seemingly acquiescent nature was when the Duke's Rolls was being serviced. It was arranged through the lady-in-waiting, Lady Jean Maxwell-Scott, and His Royal Highness's private secretary that the Duke and Duchess would share the other car. This was the first either of them had heard of it. The Duke had a dental appointment at the same time as the Duchess wanted to go to Fortnum and Mason. According to Foster, the chauffeur, they both gave their instructions at the same time. There was a pause, and the argument started.

'My teeth are more important than your visit.' Then, to the chauffeur, 'The dentist first, please, Foster.'

The dentist, who took care of many of the royal molars was always very particular about timing. He didn't like being kept waiting. The Gloucesters were now in the centre of London and the car was easily recognizable, as they quarrelled with each other through clenched teeth.

'I must have gone round Eros about four times with them at each other's throats like cat and dog. She won in the end, though. Not often you see that old bugger give way.'

It has to be admitted that the Duke was somewhat lazy. His civil duties were confined to requests from the Palace, and he would often do his best to get out of engagements or appearances. Once a year he did have to give way on a job that he hated, the Trooping of the Colour. A week before he would begin grumbling about it.

'Hope it isn't as hot as it was last year.'

'You always say that,' said the Duchess. 'It's not the weather that's to blame, it's the get-up you wear and you don't take enough exercise on a horse.'

As the day drew nearer he became ever more crotchety.

On the morning a huge crowd of tourists would gather round Kensington Palace. There was always a small group of people outside the palace, but for this occasion the numbers swelled to a throng of every sort and description, including many Americans. I thought I would give them a treat. His Royal Highness's busby had been placed in the hall by his valet, so I opened the front door and stood on the front steps displaying it. Quite a gasp went up and the cameras clicked. I didn't dare stay long in case I was caught, but it tickles me to think that in a few photograph albums scattered around the world there's a picture of me proudly labelled as the Duke of Gloucester.

A couple of minutes later down came the Duke. His valet handed him his busby, helped him in the car, straightened his uniform, and he was off, to the relief of Mr Amos and all concerned, to Buck House to mount his horse. We knew we had his return to look forward to – on horseback.

The year I was there things were almost comical. The Queen Mother was waiting at York House to greet him after the Trooping. He arrived puffing and blowing.

'Oh Harry,' she said, 'you are short of breath.'

'Yes, and so would you be.'

'But you say that every year.'

'Yes, but this year I think my horse was drunk.'

'How do you mean, drunk?'

'Well, someone must have given it a brandy or something because when the band played that thing about trombones – '

'You mean "Seventy-six Trombones"?'

'I don't know how many there were, but when they played it, the bloody horse went berserk, started to dance backwards and forwards. I had the devil's own job controlling it.'

Her Majesty stifled a laugh.

The Duchess, family and friends came in and I had to serve sherry.

Then Prince William put his oar in. 'Don't you wish, Father, that you were one of those lining the route, enjoying the sunshine and sucking ice lollies?'

'I'd steer clear of the whole bloody business if I were there.'

That mention of lollies sparked off something in the Duchess. 'That reminds me, ask the cook to prepare lemon iced sorbets for dinner.'

The Duke burst out, 'I can't stay in this uniform any longer. Russell, see if my bath is ready.' It was, and when he had emerged, changed, he was in a better mood. 'Well that bloody show's over for another year. Perhaps I can find myself indisposed next year.' He couldn't and the whole procedure, I understand, went on as usual.

The Duke watched a lot of television. Strangely, he was fond of children's programmes. To see his stern figure, one wouldn't think he was young at heart, but he didn't mind who knew it. One afternoon the front door bell went unexpectedly. When I opened it, there was Olav, King of Norway. The remaining monarchs in Europe are much more informal than ours; some of them even ride about on bicycles.

'You know who I am?' Olav asked.

'Yes, your Majesty,' I replied. I mentioned that I had had the honour to serve him at Kensington Palace.

'Is the Duke at home?' I told him he was and showed him into the Chinese Room. Then, going to the Duke's sitting room, I explained who was there. I noticed that he was watching 'Popeye the Sailor'.

'Offer him a pot of tea and ask if he minds waiting a few minutes,' the Duke said. I returned and did as he instructed. Olav accepted.

'He won't be long,' I told him.

'Why, has he got a meeting?'

'No, he's watching the television.'

'The news, or something particular?'

'Well, as a matter of fact, your Majesty, he was watching "Popeye".'

With that Olav guffawed. 'It's one of my favourites too,' he admitted.

My duties with the Gloucesters brought me into constant contact with the secretaries and ladies-in-waiting. I would be told who was coming, what food was to be served. I had to make adequate provision for cars and any special purchases, including such things as cigarettes and cigars. It was more of an administrative job than I had been accustomed to, though I still greeted guests at the door. As with Princess Marina there was the same procedure for the Queen and Queen Mother with the doors already open. Since Buckingham Palace and St James's Palace were so near, I had hardly put the phone down when they were with us. One unexpected duty fell on me that caused a scene with His Royal Highness. Amos, the valet, had to spend a few days in hospital. It was nothing serious and he was able to get there under his own steam. Before he left he went through his duties with me, ending by saying that whenever anything had to be packed it had to be wrapped in tissue paper. This struck me as footling. I think we used more tissue paper than a large store did.

'I'm not playing around with that stuff, sheer waste of money and effort. He'll have to make do with newspaper and like it. I'll use the *Mirror*, that's his favourite.'

'He won't like it, he won't like it a bit,' said Amos, and we had quite a barney over it.

That weekend I stuck to my guns. When the Duke came back, he dined alone that night and I noticed that his attitude towards me was frosty. I thought I had better have it out with him straightaway.

'Is anything the matter, your Royal Highness?'

'Tissue paper's the matter, Russell.'

I left it at that and so did the Duke, but he continued to sulk, glaring at the wall. Suddenly, he picked up a fork and threw it across the room. He behaved like a little child who couldn't get his own way. After a moment or two he said, 'Aren't you going to pick it up?'

'No,' I said. 'That's the footmen's job.' It was like 'Sam and his Musket' in the Stanley Holloway monologue. This made him more evil tempered and the meal ended with him in the blackest of moods.

A happier occasion was the staff ball held at Buckingham Palace just before Christmas. Certain senior servants attended, as did some of those who served them, like Mr Lunn of Fortnum's. It was from eight to one o'clock and was in the red and gold state ballroom, with mirrors all the way round, so that you could see yourself as you danced. Some of us took a turn with one of the royals. To my delight, happiness and trepidation, I was chosen to partner the Queen Mother for one dance at eleven o'clock. I could choose which one I wanted and selected a foxtrot at which I was likely to make less blunders. At eleven precisely I made my way over to her. 'Are you ready, your Majesty?' I asked. She was and the time seemed to go all too quickly. Although she must have gone through the same litany with each of her partners, she was as charming as her reputation. She asked me what I was going to do for Christmas, and I told her that I would be spending it with my wife and young son Ian. She danced easily and I'm glad to say I didn't disgrace myself and we chatted about families while we covered the floor. I escorted her back and then sat about relaxing and enjoying myself. Prince Philip seemed to be having a whale of a time. Shirley danced with him in a Paul Jones, which made her evening. It was indeed a splendid do and one which we shall always remember.

Like the Duchess, His Royal Highness didn't care for publicity. On one occasion he had to have his photo taken for

24th October 19 61

Peter J. Russell has been Butler at York House for one year. He is an honest, energetic young man of sober habits, who is only leaving The Duke of Gloucester's service owing to staff re-organisation.

He is joining the service of The Duke of Kent, and I wish him every success in the future.

Simon Bland.

My reference on leaving the Gloucesters

some event, and Cecil Beaton came to take it.

'That's that fella with the floppy hat, isn't it?' On being told that it was, he was disgruntled. 'Can't stand the man. Never stops talking in a funny voice. Bloody suspicious, I think.'

Whether it affected Cecil Beaton or not, he didn't show it. He was his usual breezy self, chattering away to grunts from the Duke.

The Duke, however, would often natter himself at titbits, particularly the juicy things he read in the *Mirror*. He saw a piece about battered wives and remarked upon it.

'I see people have been battering their women.'

'Have they, Harry? How interesting,' answered the Duchess.

'Extraordinary what men get up to these days.'

'It certainly is,' said Her Royal Highness, and one could detect the irony in her voice.

'I suppose they always have, since the Stone Age and all that. Still, one doesn't expect it today. Used to drag them along by the hair, I believe.'

'How very painful.'

'Yes, but women get used to anything.'

'I don't think I'd ever get used to it.'

'Not much of a chance for us to try it.'

'Hardly possible. The servants would see.'

I went into the kitchen and told them that the Duke was wanting to swing the Duchess round by the hair; everyone was most intrigued and laughed roundly when I explained.

He had his extraordinary moments. He could be talking to the Duchess and suddenly break off. For example, one day, he stopped in his tracks and said, 'Russell, that piece of jade is not in its correct place. It should be on the right of the letter sealer, and you've got it on the left. I've been looking at it for years and I like things to be the same. Please see that it's moved.'

I was not the only one to blunder. One day the lady's maid

was going up to Barnwell with Her Royal Highness for an overnight stay, using the Duchess's car. The Duchess decided to take a case with her, and the lady's maid also took some things. They were going along when the car boot opened. They looked back, and seeing what had happened, stopped to find that two small cases, one the Duchess's and one the lady's maid's, had fallen out, scattering the contents on the road. It must have been a strange sight, the pair of them sorting their things out in the middle of the road, their jumpers mixed up with knickers and other underwear. When the Duke heard the story, he guffawed until the tears ran down his cheeks.

After many months, Her Royal Highness suddenly showed an interest in our flat and the baby, and asked if she could come up at half past six that evening. Shirley got things ready. The Duchess seemed to enjoy her visit 'downstairs'. She went into the kitchen. 'What is that?' she asked. Shirley explained that it was our kitchen stove. We were astonished. It seemed evident that either she had never seen a stove before, or she'd never seen a modern one. She then saw the baby.

'Delightful creatures when they're asleep. Does he get enough fresh air?'

'Yes, your Royal Highness. We walk him in St James's Park twice a day if it is not raining.'

'Do you get any help?'

'Our mothers are constant visitors.'

Finally she remarked on the size of the place.

I quipped, 'We're thinking of taking in lodgers,' I said.

The Duchess seemed to think this a great joke.

Our eating habits were strange. Often I would take my dinner up to the flat and add it to whatever Shirley had cooked, and I was regularly able to provide fresh fruit or other tasty bits and pieces.

During the time I was with the Gloucesters, there was continuous coming and going of staff. I took it to be the changing times. If things were bad in London, they were worse in the country. Who was going to cut themselves off from town life? It became difficult to replace staff. The Duchess noticed it and said to His Royal Highness, 'Don't you think the answer to the problem is to recruit members of the ATS?'

The Duke snorted in reply, 'It certainly wouldn't. Think what some busybody would make of it in the Commons.'

So housemaids, cooks and footmen came and went in rapid succession. Shirley began complaining about the baby not getting enough air; she had to carry him up and down the stairs and he was now getting heavier. Although we had been happy for well over two years with the Gloucesters, we began to think about the future. Then came a break. I heard that the Duke of Kent needed a butler/valet and there was a cottage going with the job. This seemed to be the answer to our problems. I wouldn't be letting the Duke and Duchess down as Amos wanted my job and needed more accommodation for himself and his wife, so I knew I could pursue my inquiries without giving offence. I approached the Kents who I must say were delighted, offering me £100 a year more than my old wages. So the situation resolved itself easily and all were happy. The Duke and Duchess gave me a framed signed photograph of themselves and once again it was up sticks for the Russells.

NINE

Moving back to Coppins was like going home. We had the same removal men and the same kind of banter, only worse.

'Another royal duke, though the same bleedin' palace.'

That remark was flattering to Coppins, which could scarcely be described as palatial.

'Part of the Crown Jewels wiv yer, I shouldn't wonder.'

'He's grown up since we first came 'ere, eh, Harry?'

'Yes, it's all that good food he's getting, I reckon.'

And so it went on.

Our cottage had previously been Bysouth's, so I felt as though I really was stepping into his shoes. It seemed like a dream house to Shirley. It was semidetached, with a very large garden, which I viewed with some trepidation as it was going to be my job to look after it. Inside the front door there was a hall, then a lounge; there was also a dining room with the kitchen leading off. Outside the back door there was a walk-in coal house. There was no central heating; we had to make do with an eccentric old boiler. Upstairs there were three good-sized bedrooms and a bathroom with an old bath on four feet, rather like a piece of Queen Anne period furniture. I often tried to picture Bysouth in it, singing one of his arias.

When we had unpacked, I called at the main house and the

Duke introduced me to the young Duchess. Actually I had met her before, at Princess Alexandra's party when it had been noticeable that she spent much of the time with his young Royal Highness. Friendship ripened to love and they were married in 1961 in York Minster. The Duke hadn't cared for this apparently; he would have preferred Westminster Abbey, near to his friends and family. He had not been feeling too well either, so travelling all that distance hadn't suited him. When the young Duke married, Marina had left Coppins to live at Kensington Palace with Michael and Alexandra.

The Duke and I fell easily into the old ways. My duties were comparatively light as he was with his regiment for most of the week, except for the occasional official appearance. He had a batman/valet at his quarters, but I am glad to say he never compared the way we each did things.

The new Duchess was the only daughter of Colonel Sir William Worsley; and she had three brothers. Sir William was the third baronet, and Lord Lieutenant of the North Riding of Yorkshire, President of Yorkshire Cricket Club, and President of the MCC from 1961 to 1962. He lived at Hovingham House, and was a bluff, friendly old soul who always had a word for us. Lady Worsley was a quiet, charming woman. She always wanted a pot of tea the moment she arrived anywhere. Although she suffered from arthritis and was obviously in pain, she didn't make a song and dance about it.

Although the Duke was away so much, the young Duchess seemed to find plenty to occupy herself with. She chatted to the cook, Elsa, arranged simple lunches and entertained her friends frequently. The house hummed with youth.

However, she was not yet completely at ease. She had never had to handle a staff before. She had obviously grown up with servants around, but seemed more at home sitting on the kitchen table chatting to them than giving orders. I was not the only one to notice this; Princess Marina gave her advice and the change in her manner and the confidence she gained were quickly noticeable. This pleased everyone, staff as well, for one expects things to go on in the customary manner. I suppose the old maxim about people feeling comfortable and happier 'in their place' is true.

Life, for me at any rate, was not so formal as before. With young people abounding it couldn't be. The Duke and Duchess were very much wrapped up in themselves and in the happiness of starting a family. At weekends the Duke would take pleasure in painting some of the old furniture for the day nursery. When I first caught him with a paintbrush in his hand, I exclaimed, 'Good heavens, I never thought I would live to see the day.'

He smiled and replied, 'We've all got to make some contribution.'

I took that to mean me too, and it was rather charming when he replied to my offer of help with, 'It seems a good idea, but I'll have to speak to the Duchess first. If she agrees, then we'll do it.'

On the other side of the coin, the Duchess would say, 'Mm, mm, I think we'll have to leave that decision to the Duke. If he agrees, then we'll go ahead with it.' They were just like any other young couple in many ways.

I don't know if the need to breed is catching, but Shirley announced that she too was pregnant. When I told the Kents they seemed as excited about it as we were. It was also announced that Princess Alexandra was engaged to Angus Ogilvy, which, whether or not it had been known to the royals, had been common gossip in the servants' hall for some time. Personal observation is usually more reliable than the printed word, and lady's maids, dailies and the like see things for themselves and enjoy comparing notes, which may or may not be complimentary.

There was one sadness in my life. My mother was seriously ill and it was apparent that she had not very long to live. This news too had to be passed on to the Kents, who were sympathetic and were prepared to make sacrifices so that I could see her more often. Once again Ma Hawkings was a tower of strength. She was in and out of Mum's house, preparing all her meals and looking after her in every way. She was an inspiration to the whole street and rallied a series of visitors to take Mum's mind off what was now becoming constant pain.

Shortly after we moved to Coppins, Shirley had a knock at the door and opened it to find Princess Marina, who had called to welcome her. At first Shirley was thrown, but the Princess was charm itself, admired Ian and remarked on his fine head of hair. Then she asked if she could hold him to feel his weight. She inquired what Shirley wanted him to be. This took Shirley unawares, so she simply answered, 'Successful.' I mention this because, had Marina seen the baby at Kensington Palace, she would have paid no attention to him, but in our own home she behaved like any ordinary person.

When we had been there a few weeks, I asked if we could have the cottage decorated. This caused some humming and hawing as the money had to be found from the Duke's own pocket. It was eventually agreed, though he asked me to get it done as cheaply as possible.

By now I had introduced Shirley to Iver. Many of the village people remembered me and we were both given a right royal welcome. So, on all fronts, we soon felt happily settled.

It was not long before I bought a secondhand car. It looked exactly what it was – an old banger – but went like a bomb. Now we could travel around the countryside, which gave us a deal of pleasure. The Duke, however, wasn't so pleased with the car, or with me, when I rammed his garage doors and nearly knocked them into his Jaguar. My apologies then didn't cut much mustard. Strangely, the car didn't suffer. Things were made to last in those days, even old bangers.

On this new appointment it was to the tailor again for me. I didn't order a tail coat this time, but I got two pairs of striped trousers, a black short jacket, half a dozen shirts, a black waistcoat and tie, and a suit and jacket of my own choice.

The tailor, Davis, knew me well by now, and I only had to ask for something and it was forthcoming. I managed to assemble quite a good wardrobe. The Duke would give me ties he didn't want, and Marina presented me with a pair of cufflinks with the letter 'E' on them, as I was now looking after her son. One extraordinary piece of luck came my way. Marina and her maid were going through some old clothes and they found George VI's blue velvet smoking jacket. On his death certain items of clothing had been given to the Kent family. Marina had kept it for the Duke, but by the time he was old enough to wear it he had broadened out and it was no use to him. With almost naive generosity she offered it to me, and I quickly accepted it. Velvet jackets were just beginning to become fashionable. I took it to Davis, who removed the silk facings, and relined and refitted it for me, all for free. So, to this day, I wear a king's jacket.

Our nearest neighbour on the estate was the Countess Poplewska-Koziell, or Madame Pop, as she was known. She was the daughter of the Baroness de Stoeckl. The Baroness had been born in Paris in 1874, of Irish parents. In 1892 she married Baron Alexander de Stoeckl, son of Baron Edouard de Stoeckl, who, as Russian Minister Plenipotentiary to the United States, had been responsible for negotiating the sale of Alaska for £7,200,000 in 1857.

Baron Alexander became equerry to the Grand Duke Michael Mihailovitch, and later Comptroller to the Grand Duke George. He was eventually appointed Chamberlain to the Tsar, and the Baroness became a lady at the Tsarina's court and her daughter Zoë – Madame Pop – a *demoiselle d'honneur* to the Tsarina. In this entourage they moved in royal circles all over Europe.

After the Russian Revolution they were exiled and between the wars the Baroness worked as an assistant in a gown shop in Knightsbridge. In 1939, with Poland soon to be invaded by Germany, the Baroness, worried about her family's safety, had an audience with King George VI. The

King's brother, the former Duke of Kent, offered them servants' cottages on the Coppins estate, which is how they came to be our neighbours. So, far removed from the palatial homes in tsarist circles, they settled in to a simpler existence. Marina made them very welcome and after the Duke's death relied on them for company. When lonely, she would often lunch with either the Baroness or Madame Pop, for they shared memories of prewar Europe.

Although now in reduced circumstances, they tried to maintain the standards they had enjoyed thirty or forty years earlier. They dined at eight, and their dining table – ordinary oak, not rosewood or mahogany – was laid with place mats and finger bowls, and four candles. They still retained the services of Marisha, their Polish cook, who slept in the box room. The kitchen was small, and although only ten feet away from the lounge, had a servants' bell in operation.

When I first met the Baroness in 1955, she was living in the cottage adjoining Bysouth's. (Her daughter and son-in-law, Count Poplewska-Koziell, and their two sons, Vincent and Alexander, lived in a detached cottage close by.) At the age of seventy-eight, she had been, in her own words, 'ready for the more sober enjoyments of middle age', and wrote her memoirs, *Not All Vanity*, to escape the ennui of needlework, which her maid constantly insisted was the only fitting occupation for her.

When I returned to Coppins in the early sixties I used to drive the Baroness on my afternoons off through Windsor Great Park to visit her old Friend Mrs Sassoon, who by now was in her nineties. Although her black baby Austin Seven was far removed from the Mercedes she had once been used to, I would open and close the door for her, drape the rug over her knees, and before we started off would ask, 'Are you comfortable, your Grace?'

'Oh, my dear,' she would answer, 'that address of yours reminds me of the great entries I used to make on state occasions when I accompanied the Tsarina.'

She always sat beside me in the front, addressing me as 'my dear' and telling me of the grandeur of the pre-First World War Russian court and of the events leading up to the Revolution. She maintained that Anastasia did not survive and when I went back home my mother and Ma Hawkings would be most intrigued to hear about all this over tea and cream buns. Ma Hawkings would, in turn, regale her fellow customers while queueing for the weekend joint at the local butcher's. Both the Baroness and Madame Pop met my mother and Ma Hawkings, who felt at long last that they had met history face to face.

Years later, in July 1974, I was sitting with Madame Pop, enjoying one of her large gin and tonics. By this time her younger son Alexander, her husband the Count, her mother the Baroness, and Princess Marina had all died. She was now very lonely; her elder son Vincent was married and living in Ireland and, although he kept in close contact with her, she only had Marisha to keep her company. She pressed the bell to the kitchen and Marisha came in and shook my hand. Then, at Madame Pop's bidding, she brought two books which Madame Pop signed for me. Not long afterwards Madame Pop died, so I treasure those books greatly.

Marisha returned to Poland in 1980 to finish her days there, forty years after she had left. Ironically she returned to a Poland that was short of food and in as bad a state as it had been when she first left it so long ago.

Recently I received two letters from Vincent, thanking me for reminding him of the past and the days of his grandmother and her twenty-three cats, one of which, called Chikita, was always to be found curled up on our couch when I was butler with the Kents at Coppins in the sixties.

With the Duchess expecting a baby, Princess Marina, always anxious to see how her daughter-in-law was progressing, was a regular visitor to Coppins. She also knew about Shirley and about my mother's illness and never forgot to ask how they both were. Although she was busy with affairs of

State, the Queen made time to come down occasionally, and there were regular phone calls from Buckingham Palace to keep up with the state of play. Indeed, the phone never seemed to stop ringing. Sir William and Lady Worsley were always on the line, and there were calls from one of the Duchess's brothers, in Canada.

Then came some news which, though inevitable, I had been looking forward to like a sick headache: a nanny was to be appointed. I had not yet had any direct experience of a nanny in a household, but I had heard about them and nothing I had been told made me anything but apprehensive. The one exception, I had been assured, was Nanny Lightbody, who had looked after Prince Charles and Princess Anne, and whom I found charming and easy to talk to. All the others, apparently, were a pain in the neck. They required special treatment and were more demanding than the rest of the household put together. It was obvious what we were in for: the Duke put as much work into getting her room ready as he had done for his forthcoming baby's.

Nanny Macphearson was seen first by the private secretary and was then introduced to the Duchess, who interviewed her for nearly two hours. When I was called in to meet her I could see from Her Royal Highness's expression that she was happy with the choice and it was obvious that Nanny Macphearson had got the job – in fact, she was the only applicant. As I took her to my pantry and gave her a pot of tea, I kept saying to myself, 'Don't overestimate her, but don't underestimate her.'

She looked very much the part: smart, fit and spruce. It was difficult to pinpoint her age; she might have been anything from thirty to forty. I thought of asking her where she had previously worked, but there was something in her manner that made me change my mind. She never did volunteer this information, so I never could discover anything of her past.

She moved in soon after the interview. Her room was situated near the staff quarters; the day nursery had been

Prince Michael's bedroom, and the night nursery a guest room. She was not impressed by the house. 'Old but not practical,' she called it. When I told her that the Duke had spent a lot of time trying to make it as comfortable as possible, for both the forthcoming child and whoever was to look after it, I was rewarded with a sniff. She was dissatisfied that there was no nursery maid, which meant that she would not have enough time off. She persuaded Her Royal Highness into agreeing that she could invite her mother to Coppins as and when she wished.

Her real duties would not start until after the baby had arrived, so she spent the first weeks organizing herself, though occasionally she danced attendance on the Duchess. One of her first tasks was to stock up with the basic necessities. Farley's sent a representative round with samples of their goods. (In those days manufacturers were always keen to get the royal warrant, though many of them got sick of bearing it in the end. It wasn't worth their while to have to send a special lorry to deliver three pounds of self-raising flour, for instance, to the back door of the Palace.) The representative brought a blue and white teddy bear with Farley's name on its bottom. Well, I didn't think that royals should be asked to advertise, which would happen every time the teddy bear had its bum exposed, so I took it back to our cottage for our new baby when it arrived. When my younger son eventually tired of it, I put it in our loft at home, and there it is to this day.

Nanny and I had one major disagreement – or rather, a classic butler-versus-nanny row. I thought that she should collect her meals, wash up the plates afterwards, and bring them back to the kitchen. We really didn't have the staff to wait on her hand and foot. My request fell on stony ground, so I asked the secretary to speak to the Duchess and see if this could be arranged. He said he would do what he could. Nothing changed however, so I told Nanny I would compromise with her: I would take her food up to her if she would bring their plates down. We could toss a coin to decide who should wash up. My request was refused. I thought of mentioning it to the Duke, but he would have feigned ignorance in such matters and referred it to the Duchess. I gave up. I knew I was beaten.

When I complained to Shirley about all this, she was surprised that things were expected to go on as they had done in the past. 'You'd have thought that such people would have learned to adapt themselves to our times, in the same way as you have had to do.' While I agreed with Shirley, there was nothing I could do to alter matters. Perhaps it was because nannies were underpaid that they sought some kind of power as recompense, or perhaps it was because they were working for royals that they assumed a similar status for themselves. Whatever it was, it was damned inconvenient. In any case, I didn't have time to mope about it for suddenly someone hit us like a human bombshell.

She came in the form of a Sister – not to be confused with a nanny – and she was an experienced midwife. Sister Howell – or Flappers, as we nicknamed her – was responsible for the Duchess morning, noon and night. She gave the orders and everyone, including the family, obeyed. She prepared the Duchess for the birth and had everything at the ready. There were to be four doctors in attendance, but secretly Flappers viewed them with scorn; she appreciated what they had to do but deep down believed that birth attendance was a woman's job. However, she never let them see this and was courtesy itself so far as they were concerned.

We were a strange household during this period: lady's maid, living-in housemaid, Sister, Nanny, odd-man, butler/valet, and the Duke and Duchess, not to mention the cook – nine people, all with different reasons for being there. If we had been living in 1901, say, we would have had three times the staff but have been less close-knit. The butler would have been sharing the steward's room, with the lady's maid and the housemaid and odd-man in the servants' hall. Sister would have been in her room, Nanny in hers, and the Duke and Duchess in theirs.

It was Flappers who drew us all together as a team. Indeed, I could have resigned at that time and scarcely have been missed. She insisted on meeting all the servants and never forgot a name. When she first arrived, she introduced herself to the gardener. 'I'm Sister Howell, and I'm here for the next few weeks looking after Her Royal Highness, so best tomatoes, best strawberries, best of everything to keep mother happy.' She was very popular, even with the cook, who normally hadn't many good words for anyone, but who was all smiles when Flappers was around. Directly Flappers heard that Shirley was also pregnant she came to visit us. To her one mother and baby was the same as another. She gave us quite a lecture on what my wife had to do.

We had one slight problem with her. She had been given the freedom of the house, but she used the front door, which was forbidden even to Nanny. Also she ate with the Duke and Duchess, even though the Duke often wanted to talk privately with his wife. I put the problem to her. She understood completely and offered to have her dinner in her own room sometimes. That was in the early days. Later she dictated the times of Her Royal Highness's meals; the Duke and Duchess's wishes could go hang so far as she was concerned.

A bell was installed between her room and the Duchess's bedroom, and there was also a special bell for me. She gave me a list of all the people I had to ring in an emergency. The four doctors came at shorter intervals as the date of the birth grew nearer. This meant endless pots of tea, as the Worsleys and Princess Marina were also frequent visitors. They quickly adapted to the situation and accepted Flappers's rules. It was the occasional visitors who suffered most from her regimen. They would usually arrive in the afternoon and the conversation would go something like this:

'Oh, good afternoon, nurse. I wonder if you would take us up to see the Duchess.'

'I'm afraid not. She's resting.'

'Yes, but I'm sure if she knew it was us, she would want to see us'.

'I agree, so if you will wait until she is ready, I will see that she is told you are here.'

'But we've got to get back, it's a fifty-mile journey.'

'Whether you wait or not is a matter for you to decide.'

'But who will say when she is ready?'

'I shall.'

'Well, I really think – '

'I do the thinking for the Duchess at the moment. If you were the Queen, you still could not see her.'

The disgruntled guests then realized that they were not getting anywhere with Sister, and so had their tea.

After their visit, Flappers would be all hearts and flowers, praising their understanding and giving an account of how the Duchess was progressing, so it all ended happily.

When Flappers thought the baby was due, she changed into her uniform – she normally wore a day dress. We had three false alarms, each one signalled by her clothes. But at last the big day dawned. Her Royal Highess was most considerate, producing a son – Earl of St Andrews – at three in the afternoon on 26 June 1962.

From that moment Coppins went berserk. Everyone snatched a belated lunch from the kitchen, keeping the cook busy making sandwiches. Champagne was opened; this had been organized by Flappers, who insisted that I was given a glass. 'He's been such a helpful boy,' she said. The Queen was the first to be informed, then the Queen Mother, then the other royals. The Worsleys began to phone their friends, and, of course, once the press got the news all the papers and television wanted a story. The phone was going constantly. A number of visitors arrived who were allowed a minute or two with Her Royal Highness and then shooed out by Flappers, who only let in the people she thought were important. Then the Duke wished to be alone with his wife and baby son, so everyone was pushed out. There were people at the gate anxious for any bit of news, particularly the press, who cross-questioned anyone who was leaving. The village of Iver sent a bouquet of flowers – indeed, the house soon looked like a conservatory with flowers galore. Each bunch had to be listed so that letters of appreciation could be sent. And always there was Flappers at the centre of things, superintending everything and everybody. Finally there were phone calls and telegrams from Continental and transatlantic well-wishers – from Spain, Switzerland, Greece, America.

Seeing how busy I was, Flappers kept filling my glass, and recharging her own at the same time. Eventually she decided it was time for me to go home to my pregnant wife. I set out with some difficulty, so Flappers took my arm and saw me to the cottage. As she tottered back to the house, I couldn't help thinking it was a case of the blind leading the blind.

The following day we were all feeling rather the worse for wear, except the extraordinary Flappers, who was her usual bouncing self. She must have been about the only one able to think, let alone work. She had the Duchess on her feet after three days; she didn't believe in letting her patients sit around. With her departure a few days after the birth life seemed dull and ordinary again.

Shirley was nearing her time, so, before she left, Flappers gave her a lesson on how to wind a baby. Wind it? I thought she would kill it. Not content with Shirley, she lectured the whole staff, which was extremely funny as the majority of them were either past child-bearing age or had never stood a chance and were unlikely to be given the opportunity. Still, with Flappers, one didn't reason why.

Any royal couple having a baby receives so many presents it is impossible to use them all. With the birth of the Earl of St Andrews we were given a huge number of beautiful clothes for our impending baby. Among the gifts was an embroidered cot eiderdown and pillowcase in organza, which had come from Australia. The Duchess was thrilled by the set, but as she already had several, she gave it to us. She threw in a pair of bootees for good measure.

When the baby was a few weeks old, Princess Marina decided that her first grandson should visit her at Kensington Palace, which would one day be his home. What a to-do that was. The Duke at that time had an E-type Jaguar, which was not at all suitable for transporting the baby. At a rehearsal for the trip – arranged by Nanny, who had now come into her own – the Duchess's Ford Classic was found to be too low and cramped in the back. So it was decided to use Princess Marina's Rolls, which was sent down specially from London; the 'et ceteras' would follow in the Classic.

I couldn't help comparing the elaborate to-do with what my son would get when he arrived. Andrew was born on 10 August 1962 appropriately enough, in the Duchess of Kent wing in Hillingdon Hospital at a quarter past midnight. Sadly, my mother had died two months earlier so our celebration was subdued. Still, as Flappers had said, a baby is a baby, no matter where it is born. So, although there were no festivities, I sat with the lady's maid quietly consuming a bottle of champagne which I had nicked in the excitement over Lord St Andrews, and then I went to bed.

The next event was his Lordship's christening. For this the Queen loaned the music room at Buckingham Palace. The gathering was confined to relations and personal staff only, just a happy band of some sixty or seventy people – small by the royal yardstick. The Duke must have held past and present staff in some esteem for, after the ceremony, we travelled in cars to Kensington Palace where, in the green-carpeted drawing room, he introduced his own and his mother's staff to the Queen. He felt that it was only on such an occasion as this that we would have the chance of meeting Her Majesty. This was the first time that Shirley and I had been formally introduced to the Queen, although I had attended on her several times over the years. Shirley took the opportunity of mentioning that she too had just had a son Andrew, and she had quite a long conversation with Her Majesty on the subject of babies. Prince Philip stood there in his familiar pose, laughing as though the whole business were a huge joke. The Duke of Gloucester was also present. I wondered what his pronouncement had been on his favourite theme before he left. I told him that my second son had arrived, but this time under the roof of his nephew. The Duke seemed to have aged; he didn't look well and was slow in his movements. It wouldn't be long before age would make it impossible for him to ride to the Trooping, I thought at the time. At least that should be some consolation for growing old. The Duchess didn't appear to have changed. She seemed genuinely interested in our Andrew and said that she hoped to see him one day. I had a photograph which showed him in the same christening gown that we had bought from the baby show she had recommended.

Over tea the Archbishop of Canterbury came up and spoke to us. 'And who are you?' he asked. He seemed most interested in my job. Then I told him about our children, explaining that our first son was christened at St Martin-in-the-Fields by the Reverend Austen Williams, a man with a beautiful voice. We talked some more and the Archbishop wound up by saying that I must be getting increasingly tired of hearing 'All children are the same when it comes down to it.'

'Yes,' I replied. 'But some are more fortunate than others.' That threw him back on his heels and, with a quick, uneven smile, he left.

Princess Marina, wearing the inevitable hat, outshone everyone else at the party. The cake and champagne were excellent. If ever there was a time when I could have got the butler's complaint, it would have been during those weeks. I'm glad to say I was still able to take it or leave it.

In early autumn 1962 the Duke had to go on a state visit to Uganda. The country was to become self-governing, and it was decided that it should join the Commonwealth. The Ugandans, who had their own parliament and administration called the Lukiko, were proud of their links with Britain. The Kabaka (or king) was a character; he was known to the newspapers as King Freddie. He was part playboy, part serious politician. He had been to Cambridge and to his intense pride had been made an honorary captain in the Grenadier Guards. In the early 1950s he had asked for the separation of Buganda from Uganda and for its eventual independence under his leadership. His wishes were not granted. Instead he was put on a plane to England and told he would have to stay there until further notice on an allowance of £8000 a year. Both Buganda and Uganda rallied to King Freddie's cause and the billboards and banners in Uganda must have presented a comic sight, with pictures of King Freddie resplendent in his Guards tie – a black St George in combat with the British dragon. Eventually King Freddie's wishes were granted and the Duke was called upon to grant independence to King Freddie and the Lukiko.

This was to be my first time away from England and, although I accepted the Duke's invitation with alacrity, I was none the less somewhat nervous as to what I should find. The Duchess and the lady's maid were going as well, plus the normal retinue of diplomatic staff and security officers who always travel on such occasions. There was much to do before we left. It was as if I were back at school. The private secretary sent for me and lectured me. I was told I was not on holiday, even when their Royal Highnesses were, that I had to make sure that I was as well respected as they were, that if I was invited to any function I must conduct myself politely and courteously, that I must never get drunk – indeed, it was suggested that I lay off alcohol while I was there lest unfamiliarity breed contempt – that I must remember to say please and thank you to other staff and similar people. I was also instructed on whom to speak to and whom not to speak to, to make sure that all the luggage was in the right place and suitably labelled, and never to be far away from the Duke and Duchess. I was given a list of what clothing I should buy and where to get it. I was allowed two white tropical suits. (The Duke had seven outfits. For evening he wore either his number one white uniform, mess kit or tails. Short GCVO – Grand Cross of the Royal Victorian Order – sashes were to be worn with the mess kit, and long ones with more formal wear.) Finally the private secretary informed me that he had arranged tuition in all my duties with the Duke of Gloucester's butler, Amos, whom I already knew, and with Prince Philip's valet, who had travelled widely. To wind up, I expected him to ask if he could see my hands to make sure that they were clean. Then I would be allowed to go back to the classroom.

I met King Freddie in Kampala after the independence ceremony. It was a boiling hot day and he returned to the palace in an open carriage. As he descended some of the African onlookers fell to the ground, trying to kiss his feet – not to my taste at all. He just pushed them out of the way. Then, as he went into the palace, he said good morning to me.

A few minutes later a man came to stand next to me. To make conversation I said, 'Do I know you?'

He replied that he didn't think so.

'Are you the Kabaka's valet?' I asked.

He chuckled. 'I am the Kabaka.'

'Oh, I'm sorry. That's the first major boob I've committed, and we haven't been here that long.'

This made him laugh even more, so we were able to establish a good relationship from the start, but not in the way the private secretary would have suggested.

The palace was divided into two areas, one African, the other European, so their Royal Highnesses could chose which style of living they preferred. They opted for European, I'm glad to say – heaven knows what the African food might have done to my stomach.

There was something eerie, not of this world, about our surroundings. I remember having a couple of hours off and sitting quietly at the governor's residence having a drink of banana beer, the local tipple. Then the drums and chanting started up and I half expected someone to jump out of the bush and attack me.

I felt rather sorry for the Duchess on the trip. She was obviously nervous, not for herself, but she didn't want to let the Duke down in any way. She needed him to be proud of her. However, she did extremely well throughout and carried herself like a young queen.

After the independence celebrations we travelled to various places in Uganda. At the Mount Elgon Hotel, which was excellent and where we stayed two nights, the amount of food served to the Duke and Duchess was astronomical – six or seven courses. They couldn't manage it all and handed it over to Lilian, the lady's maid, and myself to dispose of. I recall an enormous baked Alaska. It had a base of sponge, covered with jam, then a layer of black cherries and pears smothered with ice cream and a meringue topping. The whole thing was baked quickly so that the meringue was crisp and hot and the ice cream in the middle still cold and solid. The Duke took a mouthful or two, then cried, 'Heavens, I can't eat any more. Take it away and do what you can with it.' It looked, and indeed was, delicious. Lilian and I shared it, and when I tell you that I never want to see a baked Alaska again, you'll understand how much I must have eaten.

The public-relations aspect of my job has always mattered to me, so when the hotel manager asked me if it was possible for their Royal Highnesses to spare a minute or two to meet the hotel staff, I put it to one of the equerries. He gave me a blunt refusal. Shortly afterwards I raised the matter with the Duke and to his credit he said, 'Of course we'll see them.' He and the Duchess made straight for the kitchen, shaking hands with everybody there. Thus, with a little effort, it is possible to generate a deal of good will. The equerry was obviously not pleased, but it is people like him and the secretariat who are out of touch with the realities of life. They forget that it is ordinary people, the tax-payers, who keep them in business.

Everything went smoothly on the tour, except for the episode of the Duke's hair lotion. On one of the plane flights it exploded and stained some of his shirts. I had to get them washed and ironed fast, which cost me a very large tip. At first the Duke didn't believe what had happened, but once he realized that it might explode again, the oil was discarded.

It reminded me of an incident at Coppins when the Duke, in a do-it-yourself mood, used the washing machine. One of his shirts came out blue. The housemaid and I went along to investigate. He showed us the packet and said, 'I used blue Daz and look what happened. I didn't think it would make the washing turn the same colour.' We explained that that couldn't be the case. Then the housemaid fished around in the machine and discovered that a pair of blue pants had been put in by mistake. I had the job of explaining, as tactfully as possible, that it was the colour that had run and not the washing powder that had turned the washing blue.

A trip to the Nile took us to a house which had originally been built for the Queen Mother on one of her visits. At first the Duke and Duchess thought it was too small for our party. I pointed out that there were many people at home who would have loved to live there all the year round, but I don't think they believed me. From there we visited a game park where we saw a variety of animals and birds – elephants, zebra and the like. The Duke and Duchess and officials went in one boat, and the staff followed in another. At night we saw a lioness and her cubs under searchlight. This was the first time I had slept under a mosquito net. There were lizards on the bedroom wall, which I didn't care for until it was explained to me that they only ate the insects.

The whole trip was like a glorified travel film. Although I have omitted the amount of work it entailed, I must say my previous training stood me in very good stead. As always after even the most enjoyable and eventful holiday, it was good to return home and settle into the family atmosphere of Coppins.

Over the years, both the Duke and Duchess gained in popularity and became more conscious of their position. They were taking an increasing part in representing royalty at public functions. The change in the Duchess was perhaps most noticeable. She took to her responsibilities like a duck to water. At that time there was a shortage of royal males, so it was with some surprise that we heard that the Duke was to be posted to Hong Kong with his regiment. The Duchess was to go with him, accompanied by Nanny and the baby St Andrews. They were all to share a flat. I couldn't help recalling the house on the Nile which they had considered too small. Military accommodation would make it seem a palace by comparison.

They were away for about a year, returning for a short visit for the wedding of Alexandra to Angus Ogilvy on 24 April 1963. Shirley and I were guests at the wedding in Westminster Abbey. Princess Marina arranged cars for all the servants who had been with the family for several y rs. It was another splendid occasion, with us mingling with family and friends. It was one of the last ceremonies when a large number of the kings and queens of Europe, those who were or had been, and those who considered they still ought to be, gathered together. I supposed Prince Charles's wedding was the nearest thing to it, though, of course, that was a different generation and crowned heads are thinner on the ground now.

While the Duke and Duchess were in Hong Kong, most of the staff were put on board wages and I was left to look after the place on full pay. There was only myself and a gardener in residence. At first I seemed to find plenty to do, but later time hung heavy. I joined the Iver dramatic society, then went as a dresser to the D'Oyly Carte company. Finally, incognito, I took on temporary jobs as butler, but avoiding any contact with the royals. Some of those I served were charming; others lived in the past and expected the servants of yesteryear; others were plain eccentric. There was a husband and wife who had eight chipolatas every Sunday morning for breakfast. She would have three and he five. She would arrange the sausages in a triangle, then take a boiled egg and cut it in half with a letter opener. She thought a knife wasn't good enough, the blade was too wide, whereas with a letter opener she could empty the shell completely. Her husband would cut his sausages into inch lengths, then pick them up and dip them in his egg. I came to the conclusion that to cope with this and other eccentricities I should need a course in psychiatry. Not that I minded working for them – so long as I knew that it was not going to last. It was quite an education – coping with a few crackpots. But I enjoyed it.

Then the time came for me to restaff the house. It wasn't easy: I was getting to the stage when second-best just would not do. Also I couldn't contemplate seeing out my time for another thirty years, finally ending up in retirement in some grace-and-favour flat amongst others of my breed, with nothing to do but discuss the past. Nor did I relish the idea of my sons growing up with the royals who would, as children, accept them as equals, but with the passing of the years would begin to feel their own position and show it. I felt this particularly in relation to my son Andrew and the Kents' son just two months older than him. I was still a royalist; indeed, my excursions into service outside had confirmed my feeling that I would never wish to work elsewhere, but I was beginning to tire of serving them. However, I do believe, that the royal family give this country some sort of backbone, for which, in times like these, we should be grateful.

It could be said, and with some truth, that I am a bit of a snob. I served people who, by virtue of birth and position, could also be described as snobs. I felt that I had become as one with them. It was inevitable that this should happen, because of the proximity in which we lived. In addition, there is the theatrical element in being in service. This appealed to me although I have not emphasized it.

For a newly married couple, being in service is an ideal way of providing a home. We could not have afforded to buy a house when we first married, and would have had to live with one of our mothers, which would not have worked. Our children also benefited materially from the life that we led. When the time came to make the break we were able to provide a proper home for them, due in part to the savings that had accumulated over the years.

So, for us it was time to make a change. One evening Shirley and I sat down and considered our future. I was by now a fair organizer; I was no time-watcher – indeed, I'd be surprised to hear of another job that required the same number of hours that I had been putting in. I was interested in and well informed about food and it was in this area that I felt I could make some contribution. So I started applying for jobs. Eventually I was successful, and was offered a position with a large catering company, which seemed ideal. It was based in Essex, but well outside London. We found a house, put down a deposit out of our savings and some money that my mother had left – quite a sum considering her circumstances – and had our mortgage accepted. It was not till everything was neatly settled that I told the Duke. He was very decent about the whole thing and understood the reasons for my leaving. So indeed did the rest of the family, including Marina. Even so, I felt somehow disloyal.

Now, nearly thirty years since I entered royal service, what has given me the greatest pleasure is that my sons have done well in the spheres they have chosen, and they have grown up into a strong sense of self. One is a qualified computer programmer, working in the City; the other is at university reading mathematics. My mortgage is fully paid up and I feel a sense of satisfaction and achievement. Strangely, though, there has been one thing missing from my life. I have continued to hanker after the job I was anxious to get away from – service – and when the opportunity offered itself, I decided to give my old skills a try again. This time around, however, I am my own boss: I work as a 'contract' butler. Essentially the

work is the same as before, but somehow I feel there is a little
more dignity to it as I now choose where I work and feel
independent of my employers. It's hard to explain. The best
of both worlds, perhaps.